BOOMER TALES

Adventures Of A
Part-Time Delinquent

By
KENT FORD

Boomer Tales
© 2020 by Kent Ford

ISBN (Print): 978-1-09832-820-7
ISBN (eBook): 978-1-09832-821-4

Prologue

Why would somebody nobody ever heard of write a memoir? That completely understandable question deserves an answer. I'm getting on in age, seventy at the start of this writing, now peering back at seventy-two, a product of the Baby Boom, that generation of Americans born in the years immediately after World War II. I've written this for a number of reasons, some reflective, others responsive to myself and others. Also to vent, express regrets, ask lingering questions. My father and mother are gone, father died in 1998, mother in 2015, as are my stepmother, in 1980, and stepfather, in 2015. I'm next in the line of generational extinction.

My father and stepfather both served in the military during wars, father in World War II and stepdad in the Korean War. I know almost nothing about their service. Most of the details and anecdotes that made up their early lives and the lives of my mother and stepmother died with them. My mother and stepfather shared brief memories now and then, usually the same stories year after year. My father and stepmother shared virtually nothing about their lives. None of my parents ever talked much about their youth, their work, their joys or regrets. I don't know what made them proud or if they felt they had failed in any way. I never asked them to tell me their stories, and because I made a career out of asking questions, it disturbs me that I didn't pry from all four of them more stories from their lives. All I have left of them, beyond a number of photographs, are superficial highlights. Their glory and their regrets, the essence of who they were, died with them. I'll never know the things that made them who they were.

Everyone has stories to tell, good and bad, uplifting and depressing, joyous and mournful. Far too many of those stories vanish along with the lessons to be learned from them and the histories of our families.

Another reason I wrote this is because my son, Justin, suggested I should. Writing these stories had occurred to me, but the thought carried along nothing to break the inertia of not writing. Justin wants to remember some of the stories I've shared at family gatherings and around the dinner or game table: Swamping my canoe in a flooded creek with nighttime approaching, terrorizing a drive-in theater, earning a combat action ribbon while absent without leave, looking a ghost in the eye at Gettysburg. Justin gave me the boost necessary to get started writing. Unfortunately, he lives too far away to prod me along.

Justin also sometimes feels a poke of curiosity about his genealogy. Many of us want to know something about who came before us in our families. Who were they? Where did they come from? How and why did we get where we are? The stories of my parents' lives beyond what brothers and sisters, aunts and uncles remember are gone. Our aging memories brew family disagreements over details. So, here's my effort.

One more reason for writing a memoir: It's entertaining to remember, mostly. Lots of people grow crusty and abrasive with age. I'm trying not to. At times, my feeble wise-acre attempts to be funny come across more as condescension. I try hard to hold my tongue, but sometimes my brutish skepticism overpowers my best effort. You won't read here any spiteful words about anyone other than myself. If something sounds nasty toward someone, it's because an effort at humor failed. Forgive me. I also ask forgiveness for any errors of omission or faulty memory.

Remembering isn't all fun, though. Telling about how I totaled a friend's car doesn't make me feel warm and fuzzy. People, even me, do boneheaded things. Those also make entertaining stories, painful as they are to tell.

My wonderful wife Sharon gets far less mention here than she should. She has filled my life since my twentieth birthday. For more than fifty years Sharon has been plunging ahead right by my side. There's been friction now and then, but little beyond routine for married people who love each other. I tend to hold my tongue when circumstances indicate imminent escalation. I've swallowed large helpings of pride and frequently clenched my teeth when I wanted badly to bark. That's poor strategy for a politician or a titan of industry, but I'm neither of those. Politicians often lead us into war, and business moguls spend a lot of time in court. Wars and lawsuits are best avoided, especially in marriage, and even more so in families. Battles have victors, but nobody wins wars. And losers carry grudges. I am and have always been happily married and embrace my extended, splintered families as best I can.

This memoir is chronological to a point. It skips most of the mundane details that made up most of my life. These stories about things that occurred during my life are for my children and their children and grandchildren. I hope they enjoy reading them, and that they learn some things to not do. This memoir can easily be read piecemeal or back to front. It has no plot.

Before you get started, I have one humble request. If you use this as a toilet companion, please store it well above the bowl so it doesn't get splattered by every male who whizzes by.

For my daughter Kathryn (Katie), my son Justin, and their children: Katie's Nate, Aleah and Karsen, and Justin's Olivia, Isaac and Elias, a marvelously mixed bag

Acknowledgements

I am thankful for the help of a number of people during this process. My wife Sharon read this manuscript, caught several mistakes and offered a number of suggestions. Other members of my family helped jog my memory and provided dates and other information. They are my brother Scott, sisters Candace LaCroix, Jackie Cowgill and Valerie Sumner.

George Swanger, a Navy friend, provided help with details about an adventure in Japan.

Members of the Columbia/Central Missouri Writers Guild read excerpts from the manuscript and offered their suggestions.

Thanks everyone!

BOOMER TALES

Adventures Of A
Part-Time Delinquent

Chapter 1

Somehow Surviving Wellsburg

Unless you had a big brother, you wouldn't do this sort of thing. I'm claiming my brother Scott told me how to do this. I put a .22 rifle bullet on the sidewalk in front of our house and smacked it with a hammer. That doesn't sound like something that would have occurred to a four-year-old without outside influence. The bullet, which probably came from Dad's work bench in the basement, went off, of course. It either hit a house up the street or fell harmlessly to earth. Dad revoked my hammer privileges.

We lived in Wellsburg, Iowa, a tiny dot near the center of the Iowa highway map. It's fifteen miles northeast of another tiny dot that represents Eldora. I squalled my first objection to the indignity of life in the hospital in Eldora, a town that comes back into this story a bit later. Wellsburg, where my family lived, like most small rural communities even today, didn't have a hospital. Eldora had the nearest one. When I came along my family consisted of my dad Harley, my mother Donna, older brother Scott and now me. Scott is a year and six months older than I. For six months after April, he's only a year older. Then October comes around and he's two years older again.

One of the few stories Mother told about my infancy was that I nearly died. My breathing became ragged and shallow one day. Dad drove Mom and me to the hospital in Eldora. Mom kept me alive during the brief trip by swinging me around by the heels in the back seat. That's what she told me. How that helped my breathing or why she thought it would, she never explained. In my imagination I see her bashing out my brains on a door handle.

Doctors determined my swollen thymus gland clogged my windpipe. Treatment involved radiating the gland, Mother said. That worked, apparently, but that radiation may have caused other medical issues twenty years later. Many people who received similar radiation treatment developed thyroid problems like me. Some died of thyroid cancer. I had two surgeries to remove thyroid lumps, one when I was in the Navy in Lemoore, California. The second procedure, because the thyroid lump returned, occurred while my own family lived in Poplar Bluff, Missouri. Neither lump tested malignant. A small, inexpensive daily pill, a medication taken by many, substitutes for my missing thyroid gland.

No Headlines

As far as I know my birth didn't create a family crisis or a newspaper headline, just some disagreement many years later. To prevent instant confusion, you need to know that like many people everywhere I have two immediate families, the Fords, my father's family, and the Stewarts, my mother's family. My in-laws consist of a family of families, which absorbed me later. I have been a part of my wife Sharon's sprawling family for fifty years. But that family's branches and twigs confuse me, and no attempt will be made here to clear that up. My father, Harley, and mother, Donna, divorced when I was still in diapers, sometime around 1950. I have no memory of living with them as a couple. Through high school in central Iowa I lived with my father and the Ford family. After graduation I went to Missouri to live with my mother and the Stewarts.

My family of Fords – not the assembly-line automobile-rich Fords nor the multitude of other Fords in the world, black and white – lived in Wellsburg when I was born on April 6, 1948. Or was it April 7? I came to learn years later that my mother swore I came into the world on April 7. She even declared that my birth certificate, with April 6 on it, is wrong. "I'm your mother," she said with enough edge in her voice to settle the issue. "I know damn good and well what day you were born on." Her exact words. Who or what to believe, my mother or my birth certificate?

My mother and I lived apart for most of my first eighteen years, during which time my birthday was April 6. Coincidentally, my father's father, Fred Ford, as crusty an old man as you'd ever care to meet, was born on April 7. I've stuck with April 6 out of habit and because that's what my birth certificate records. On the other hand, hospital people do make mistakes. Also on my birth certificate, my mother's name is written Donna Joyce Stewart. Her middle name wasn't Joyce, it was Joye. Could the date of my birth as recorded on the certificate also be wrong? It certainly could. When I get around to updating my obituary, which I've written to help out whoever has to bother with that, maybe I'll change it to: Born, April 6/7, 1948.

California Sojourn

Harley and Donna divorced before I was two. Mother took Scott and me to live with some of her family in California. One of Donna's brothers-in-law liked to tell the story about how he would take me to a local store and send me back to the cooler to get a quart of beer for him. It must have been funny, he always laughed when he told about it.

In 1951 Dad married LaVelle Bausman, who lived in Wellsburg and had babysat Scott and me. LaVelle became my mom as I grew up.

Donna had spent her childhood in north Missouri, and she soon moved back to Missouri and entered Missouri State Teachers College in Kirksville. (Over the years that school's name changed to Northeast Missouri State University and then to Truman State University.) Donna married my stepdad, Charles Robert "Bob" Stewart, in June 1952.

The Korean War broke out in the early 1950s. Bob served in the Army in Korea. The only story he ever told me about his war experience involved the trip to Korea by ship. Most of the troops, many of whom had never seen the ocean before, got seasick. When they were at chow in the ship's mess hall, with the ship rolling in the waves, food trays slid back and forth on the tables, Bob said. It was disgusting when your tray slid under your neighbor's chin and he puked in it. It really got nasty when your tray slid back to you.

Bob loved to tell stories, especially funny ones. He embellished freely and even made up some of the stories, but that just added to his fun. Bob and his brother, Bill Stewart, played baseball all over north Missouri in their youth and young adulthood. Bob played catcher. Stories about baseball at any level were his favorite.

Scott, on the right, and me with our stepmother LaVelle and father Harley on our front walk in Wellsburg, Iowa. The house across the street behind Dad sheltered a tribe of kids and one of the neighborhood moms who provided first aid for any kid in need.

Return to Iowa

Scott told me that he and I rode a train from California back to our dad, Harley, after he married LaVelle.

Dad built our house in Wellsburg. One of my earliest memories of life features his work on that house. I remember teetering along on floor joists spanning the basement. We lived in the basement while Dad hammered the house together overhead when he wasn't at work. He repaired cars in a tiny cinder-block garage on the fringe of downtown Wellsburg a few blocks from our house.

Several years earlier Dad had worked on motors in all types of vehicles, from jeeps to tanks, while in the Army during World War II. Harley never told me this, but my brother Kevin said Dad worked stateside early in the war on a special tank project. His crew tried to figure out how to stack three V-8 engines in a tank and synchronize their torque. That project ended when it became apparent that such a rig would be impossible to maintain on the battlefield. After that Dad's unit followed the infantry into Germany.

Three or four hundred people, many of them German and Dutch immigrants or their descendants, lived in Wellsburg. The American Veterans (Amvet) Hall next door to our house anchored the southeast corner of town. Scott and I roller skated in the Amvet Hall on Saturday mornings along with other kids from the area. I couldn't have been older than five or six. I fell down regularly. One time my fingers got run over. I suspect Scott. Our house being next door, Mom probably heard me holler.

One day I went into our house and found LaVelle lying on the kitchen floor whimpering. She told me to hurry next door to tell our neighbor to come over. That's all I remember about that. I suspect that was the miscarriage of my half-brother. He was named Kim, but I didn't even learn of his existence for several years. Kim is buried in the Ford family plot in the cemetery at Grundy Center, another small town near Wellsburg. Nobody ever talked to me about that event, then or later.

Haunted Playhouse

Across the street an abandoned derelict of a house haunted the inside of the curve that ran in front of the Amvet Hall next door to our house. The corner wasn't an intersection, the street passed our house and broke sharply around the lot occupied by the spooky house. That curve defined the southeast corner of town that served as a base of operations for Scott and me. The decaying house and its weedy yard provided a wonderfully treacherous playground. We discovered an abandoned honeybee hive in one of the crumbling lathe-and-plaster walls of the derelict building. We choked down sour green crabapples from a tree in the side yard and tempted gravity on a platform treehouse nailed into a tree that loomed just inside the curve. A stairway that had migrated from the side of the old house gave fast, easy access to the tree platform fashioned of doors taken from the gray ruin.

Over the years the weather and the sun had baked away every trace of any paint the house may have sported. Bricks from the crumbling chimney littered the yard on the east side of the house. A tree, just large enough for a small kid to climb, had sprouted among the bricks beside the foundation. I scooted out onto one of the tender limbs, swung back and hung by the back of my knees like we did on the monkey bars at school. The limb snapped at the trunk. One of those fallen chimney bricks broke my fall. It connected on my forehead just above my nose, squarely between my eyes.

I ran screaming across the street. Our house hadn't seen such bleeding since Dad nearly cut off his fingers on his table saw in the basement. Mom called the town doctor who rushed over from his downtown office. He determined that I didn't need stitches, and bandaged the wound. The dent in my forehead remains, if you need proof of this calamity.

That doctor took care of most of the people in and around Wellsburg. He made house calls, but he took out my tonsils in his storefront office.

Pie a la Road

Mom's mother, whom we called Grandma Bausman, or frequently simply Bausman, lived downtown. Why we called my grandmother by her last name I can't say, but it remains common in Iowa that people call friends and relatives by their last names. It must be a habit of familiarity, likely packed over from Germany. Grandma Bausman's name was Annette. She was Wellsburg's postmaster.

My stepmom, LaVelle, and her mother, Grandma Bausman, at my sister's wedding in the early 1970s.

Grandma's son, LaVelle's brother Lawrence, worked with Dad in the auto repair shop. Grandma Bausman's husband, Irl, a farmer, died young, long before I was born.

Grandma lived in an apartment over a bank on the corner of a main intersection in Wellsburg, diagonally across the street from her post office. An open staircase clung to the side of the bank, giving access to Bausman's apartment. I don't recall being frightened by those stairs at the time, but thinking about them now makes me shudder. The lower level of that building remains, but the upper level apartment where Bausman lived is gone.

We went to Grandma's apartment for Christmas and sometimes for Sunday dinner. We took dessert or some other dish. For one visit Mom made one of her delicious Boston cream pies, really more of a cake. I remember that particular visit because I dropped the pie when we got out of the car. It landed flat on its top in the gravelly road beside the car. That disappointed us. I learned to pay close attention when given responsibility, especially for dessert. None of us ever went hungry at Bausman's, even without dessert.

Grandma Bausman later moved to a little house a few blocks away from downtown. Her house sat a block up the street from the house Dad built. We no longer lived in Wellsburg when Bausman moved.

Kindergarten Cut-Up

Mom took me to my first day of kindergarten in Wellsburg. After that I walked with Scott the eight blocks to school and back, even in winter. I have few memories of my early years in school, other than playing with clay.

One day in kindergarten or first grade I was sitting backwards at my desk talking to or making faces at the kid in the seat behind me. Suddenly I got snatched up, spun around and plunked back down facing the front of the room. Whether she said anything, I don't recall, but the teacher had got my attention. That humiliating episode made a pretty fair pupil out of me until I reached about seventh grade, when like many I began to degenerate somewhat.

Feral Kids

Families next door, across the street, and nearby littered our Wellsburg neighborhood with kids who ran lose all day, some of us shoeless and barely clothed, like small-town kids all around the country in the early 1950s. Other memories of our years in Wellsburg linger in the cranial fog. A small dog in our neighborhood jumped up and bit my face, right around one of my eyes, which eye I don't recall.

A bumblebee stung me when I was playing on a belt auger in a city storage yard a couple of blocks from our house. I ran home bawling and the mother in the house across the road whose kids we ran with put some butter on the sting. Neighborhoods in small towns provided several mothers for all of the feral kids. Every house didn't have a neighborhood mother. Some folks kept their curtains drawn, others were feeble. If a household contributed a kid to the pack though, everyone knew where you could get a bandage for a scrape or butter for a bee sting.

Dad conjured wine in a stone crock in the basement. One day I went with him to check his batch. While he fussed with the crock, I laid a board against a nearby table and crawled up it. Just as I reached the tabletop, the board slipped. My teeth caught the edge of the table as I fell. Dad took me to a tooth doctor in Waterloo. The doctor said my teeth would survive, but they would remain crooked without braces. I went without braces for fifty years.

Scott Escapes Death, Barely

Scott narrowly escaped early death one day on the street in front of our house. He was five. A woman driving drunk careened around the haunted-house curve and snagged my brother with the front bumper of her car.

Scott says I was present, but I have no memory of it. Perhaps it's repressed. We were tossing mudballs with the street as no-man's land. It may have been just him against me, a fraternal conflict that continued for years. It often happened to be my misfortune that I was Scott's only available adversary. He grew up to become a Marine. No, that's not right. Scott was born a Marine, he just aged into the Corps. He has mellowed, mostly because his body hurts when he acts Marinish. When Scott goes fishing, which he does often, the fish aren't game, they're the enemy.

Anyway, Scott mounted a mudball attack just as the drunk sped around the curve. The car dragged Scott a couple of blocks up the road. His arm tangled in the bumper kept him from being run over and killed. My only memory of that event comes second-hand through a photo of Scott standing in the front doorway of our house with his arm in a cast and sling. He proudly wears scars on the bicep of the entangled arm and the knee skinned severely by the front tire of the car.

Mad Mom, Other Stuff

One time, driven by boredom, I walked a couple of blocks to a friend's house to see if he could play. I knocked on the door and knocked on the door and knocked some more. My friend's mother eventually responded. She hollered and ran me off. I don't know what I interrupted, probably a nap or something equally important. She didn't even ask me what I wanted. She just wanted me gone.

Dad made kites and kite-flying stools for Scott and me. We flew the kites in the cow pasture behind our house. Out in the middle of the pasture a windmill pumped cold, clear water into a concrete trough for cattle to drink. Kids drank out of it too when roaming nearby. The kite stools had seats and large spool attachments like fishing reels that held the string. We sat astride the stools and reeled in or out to control how high the kites flew. We didn't use the kite stools much, kite flying not being a stationary activity. Using Dad's kite-building technique, however, I made my own kites for several years.

Dad hung a musty old tarp over the pasture fence behind the house and hit golf balls into it. That didn't last long though. Golf balls will shred a tarp. Dad raised rabbits in hutches behind the house. We ate them. We also ate chickens Dad butchered in the backyard. He chopped off their heads then tossed them on the ground where they flopped around and ran amok headless for a minute or two.

Dad had a black Labrador retriever named Jack, a good dog.

During patrols around the neighborhood, kids picked up pop bottles from the ditches where people had thrown them from their cars. (At some point south of Wellsburg, but not too many miles, people don't drink pop, they drink soda. Same drink.) Lots of people threw trash out their car windows. Anti-littering campaigns lurked in the future. The gas station and grocery store downtown gave two cents for each bottle brought in.

If you paid attention and got there first after a Friday or Saturday night, a kid could haul in a wagonload of bottles. That took considerable work, though. I counted it a good haul if I could redeem ten or twenty cents worth.

Wheelchair Is Frightening

A boy named Leo lived across the street, next door to the abandoned house on the corner. Polio hit Leo hard. He used a wheelchair and moved with difficulty. Leo could talk in a hoarse croak, but I couldn't understand him most of the time. He was several years older than Scott and me, and I had a little kid's fear of him. That was unfortunate. Scott told me years later that Leo was a nice guy and that he liked sitting outside with neighborhood kids around. Leo lived for many years. It makes me sad that I was so frightened of him.

Polio crippled many children around the world during summers in the first half of the 20th Century. Nobody knew what caused it. Swimming pools and movie theaters were closed during the polio season. In some victims, polio weakened muscles used to breathe. Those unfortunates survived with the aid of a horrifying machine called an iron lung that enclosed the entire body of the kid. Only his head stuck out. Until Dr. Jonas Salk developed a vaccine in the mid-50s, families lived in fear of the horrible disease. The Salk vaccine has virtually eliminated polio.

Easy Come, Easy Go

Uncle Lawrence and his wife, my Aunt Donna, came by our house early one Sunday morning. Uncle Lawrence gave me a quarter. I don't think I'd ever had a quarter before. Big money. It must have been a special Sunday, or maybe Uncle Lawrence had got lucky that morning, or maybe he wanted to be my favorite uncle. Uncle Lawrence had never before indicated that I was anyone special, so it must have been the day that induced his generosity. Maybe it was my birthday. I put the quarter into my pocket along with the nickel Mom gave me for Sunday School offering.

At Sunday School the plate came past and I put in my offering with no thought about where my nickel would go or what good it would do for anyone. It's just what you did, put your money in the plate. A bit later, back at home, I reached into my pocket to admire once again the quarter Uncle Lawrence had given me. I pulled out a nickel. I wanted to rush back to church and demand my quarter back! I had no idea what I would do with that quarter, but I knew I wanted it instead of that nickel.

Uncle Lawrence, left, and Dad, right, in their shop in downtown Wellsburg.

We Get Television

One day, probably in 1955 or '56, a tall antenna appeared rising up the side of our house. It had not been there when I went to school that morning. I hurried inside. We finally had a television set! Reception stunk, the nearest stations being many miles away from Wellsburg, probably in Waterloo or Des Moines, but we could watch one or two fuzzy channels. My favorite shows were Howdy Doody, The Lone Ranger and The Cisco Kid..

Television watching became a privilege that could be revoked for misbehavior or dangled as incentive to be good. One day Mom made split pea soup for supper. My adolescent palate had not developed to the point where I could choke down pea soup, even with the threat that I could not leave the table until I cleaned my bowl. While the family sat in the living room laughing at the TV set, I sat at the table, tears dripping into my congealing green dinner.

We didn't get a color television for many more years. The first color program I saw was "Bonanza" at a friend's house in Grundy Center. How amazing it was to watch Lorne Greene and his three rancher sons riding their horses amid the colorful landscape of the Ponderosa. It looked like the actual frontier to me.

Over the years I came to accept that any beautiful young woman who had the misfortune of falling in love with Adam, Hoss, Little Joe – or even the patriarch, Ben Cartwright for that matter – was doomed to perish before the end of the episode. You could bank on it. She'd be in the ground before 8 p.m. The only suspense was guessing what would cause the demise of the unfortunate sweetheart, a buckboard accident, a stray bullet from a saloon drunk or an awful disease that swept the countryside.

Our Family Grows

My half-sister Candace joined the clan on September 28, 1953. Two weeks shy of a year later, on September 11, 1954, half-brother Kevin came along. Times were changing in the Ford house, including the location of the house. We moved to Grundy Center about this time, when I was seven.

Chapter 2

Change of Scenery

The three towns of my early childhood, Wellsburg, Eldora and Grundy Center, form a neat triangle on the Iowa map, with Wellsburg at the northern apex. Eldora sits on the west angle of the triangle, Grundy Center straight east on the third point. Highway 175 connects Eldora and Grundy Center. You turn north off of 175 onto a county highway to get to Wellsburg.

We moved the thirteen miles from Wellsburg to Grundy Center into a nondescript two-story rental. It sat on a corner three blocks south of Highway 175, which runs through town and serves as main street. The house had a large open kitchen, a dining room and a living room on the bottom floor and bedrooms on the upper level. We lived four blocks east of the elementary school. A detached garage provided Dad a place to do his wood work, which included the manufacture of a boat for duck hunting. If Dad ever took his heavy-but-sleek boat to the water, I don't know. We never ate any ducks.

A furnace that seemed huge to me took up much of the basement. Dad fed all kinds of wood into that furnace in winter, including pieces of old utility poles he cut up with a buck saw after somehow hauling them home. I don't know where Dad got the poles, but he didn't get arrested. One day dad emerged from the garage with an armload of wood to carry down to the furnace. His timing, or mine, proved poor. A football I had just punted smacked him in the face. Dad scowled at me fiercely, but the load of firewood prevented pursuit.

Shared Bedrooms

Scott and I shared a bedroom in every house we lived in until the family moved to Grinnell after my sophomore year of high school. Scott remained in Grundy Center after he graduated in 1964. From our second-floor bedroom in our first house in Grundy, we sometimes looked at the sky at night. Scott showed me how to pick out the Big and Little Dippers. We watched a comet out that window. Two bright comets passed by within a month of each other in the spring of 1957.

We lived in Grundy Center during most of my youth. Grundy, the informal name used by the 2,500 townspeople and others in the region, lies in the center of Grundy County on a line between Waterloo to the northeast and Marshalltown to the southwest. Grundy County has some of the richest soil on the planet, much of it flat. The county contributes greatly to Iowa's ranking as one of the top corn-producing states year after year. In late summer you can't see far beyond the ditches that border rural roads. Corn stalks from eight-to-ten feet tall block your view mile after mile. In winter you see mile after mile of flat or gently rolling hills of black dirt when snow doesn't cover the ground, a dreary scene either way, unless you own the land.

Laying Down the Law

Dad played golf when he could, which wasn't often, but he enjoyed the game. His bag and clubs were always easily accessible. I got out one of his clubs and a ball one day and went into the yard beside the house. It didn't take long for me to launch the ball into the street, from where it caromed through the front door window of a neighbor's house.

Dad paid to replace a number of windows in the neighborhoods we occupied through the years. Scott and I both contributed to the count. Dad finally laid down the law, "No more broken windows!" In life, outcomes don't always match expectations. Not a week after Dad declared the moratorium on window breaking, I was at bat in a game of workup softball in a friend's yard two blocks from home. I smacked a liner into center field, which might have been sixty feet from home plate. The ball stuck between a storm window and interior window of the house next door, breaking them both. My memory of the consequences of that ground-rule double resides in the repressed section of my brain.

A family named Miller, a man and woman and two adopted girls, both a bit younger than me but old enough to be playmates, lived across the street. Because the girls and I played together, Mrs. Miller tolerated my presence in her house on many a day after school. She gave the girls and me Oreo cookies and milk while we watched The Mouseketeers on television. During a couple of summers, I cut the Miller's grass in exchange for them buying me a $15 season pass to the town swimming pool. The cranky reel push mower I used made me wish I'd turned down the deal.

Shower in the Nude

Grundy Center had an above-ground municipal swimming pool built through the Works Progress Administration (WPA) during the Great Depression in the 1930s. The WPA was among the "big government" programs that President Franklin Roosevelt strong-armed through Congress. Conservatives claim Roosevelt's programs like the WPA had little to do with ending the Depression. World War II did that, they say. That misses the point. Those programs weren't intended to end the Depression. The WPA and other new government programs gave people jobs and paychecks, which put food on their dinner plates.

Thousands of communities across the country had new WPA facilities like Grundy's swimming pool. Swimmers entered the oval-shaped building through a small lobby on one of the narrow ends. Changing areas and shower rooms, boys to the right and girls to the left, curved around the perimeter of the concrete and cinder-block structure. Steps near the back led up to the pale blue and green escape from the heat of the Central Iowa summer. A sign behind the front counter directed swimmers to "Take a shower in the nude" before entering the water. Nobody ever did that. Younger kids asked, "Where's the nude?"

Two tennis courts beside the pool provided handy places to lie in the sun and warm up after time in the always-frigid water in the pool. If you had a nickel you could get a soft-serve ice cream cone from Smitty's Drive-in on the far side of the tennis courts. Fifteen cents could get you a small paper basket full of Smitty's salty, greasy-sweet curly fries, everyone's favorite.

A few times during the summer Dad declared on a Sunday evening that we were "going for a ride." These occasional expeditions involved all of us piling into whatever car we happened to have at the time and Dad driving slowly around town, just looking. Rides excited us kids because they usually included a stop at Smitty's for nickel cones.

The street between our house and the Millers rose gently to the west. A home for the elderly occupied a lot on the corner at the top of the hill on the Miller's side of the street. A porch wrapped around the street sides of the home. During warm weather the residents, wrapped in blankets, sat outside in rocking chairs. Another block in that direction was the junior high school, formerly the high school, and another block farther the elementary school.

Sledding Headquarters

The elementary school sat on the highest spot in town. The playground on the side of the school toward our house sloped downward. In winter that hill became the go-to spot for sledding. Dozens of kids took their sleds to school with them. Most were the kind of sled with two steel runners. You could steer with your hands if you rode on your belly or with your feet if you sat up. We were belly floppers. You got the most exciting ride by holding your sled in front of you, running up to the edge of the hill and flinging yourself headlong down the slope, flopping onto your belly on your sled. With the low center of gravity, you could make your sled swoop and dodge, causing or avoiding crashes. Pile-ups occurred, but we were padded.

Before class, during recess and after school the hillside teemed with bundled-up, mittened kids. It didn't take long for sled traffic to pack fresh snow into a slick track. I could ride all the way to the grounds of the junior high school if it happened to be my last ride of the day. It was on my way home. The hill provided Grundy Center kids with an adventure we thought unmatched anywhere in the county. Seeing the hill years later, barren of snowpack, the gentleness of its slope surprised me. That couldn't possibly be the same hill that had provided winter thrills in my youth. The school building came down long ago.

Engineering Miscalculation

Sleds were for winter fun. A bicycle got me around town the rest of the time, in summer to the swimming pool. One day I crafted a small ramp out of pieces of a wooden orange crate I scavenged from behind the grocery store up the street. I placed the ramp in the center of the street between our house and the Millers and rode up the street toward the old folks' home. With enough speed, I thought, that ramp will launch me down the road a few feet. That's exactly what it did. Unfortunately, it didn't launch my bike along with me. The ramp might as well have been a stone wall. Various of my appendages got scraped up some. Realizing quickly that I had done a profoundly stupid thing, I didn't complain much about my injuries.

Kitchen Accessories

A radio sat on a kitchen counter. Mom laughed when "You Ain't Nothin' but a Hound Dog" played and I hopped and shimmied around the kitchen while drying the supper dishes. The song was funny, but I liked it a lot. A young rock-and-roll singer, Elvis Presley, released his cover of the goofy hit in 1956. Several years later my stepdad Bob Stewart assured me that songs like "Hound Dog" weren't released, they escaped.

Another thing we had in the kitchen for a while was a cage with a chicken in it. Popular during those years were chicks dyed blue, pink or green for Easter. Somebody in our family, one or another of the kids, possibly me, thought it would be fun to have one of those Easter-dyed chicks.

We got a birdcage from Grandma and Grandpa Ford, who lived four blocks up around the corner. For years they kept canaries in their house, enjoying the cheery music they made. Chickens don't remain chicks, nor do they stay Easter-dyed, very long. We soon had a full-grown chicken trapped in a canary cage in our kitchen. Common sense prevailed upon somebody and the chicken went away. We had relatives on Dad's side of the family who lived on a farm near Grundy. That may be where the chicken went, or maybe Dad wrung its neck in the garage and we ate it for Sunday dinner.

A man driving a special van put a gallon of milk in a silver box just outside our door a couple of times a week. If you put a note in the box, the milkman would leave butter.

First Kiss

My third-grade teacher, whom I had a crush on, got married in a nearby town. She invited her pupils to attend the ceremony. One or two of my classmates and I went to the wedding. One of the other kid's dad drove. Our teacher looked even more beautiful than usual. What the groom looked like,

I haven't a clue. He could have been green and bald. I wouldn't have noticed. It was my first wedding. The brevity of the ceremony surprised me.

When the bride and groom were greeting all of the guests after the "I Dos," my teacher put her hands on my cheeks, bent over and kissed me right on the lips. She smelled as good as she looked. I blushed. My classmates and I jabbered about the wedding all the way home. Thinking about that kiss floated me through the next week or two. If I had ever been kissed before by a woman not in my family, it must not have impressed me.

Chapter 3

Trouble in Eldora

A fter we had been in Grundy Center for a couple of years, Dad got a job in Eldora, the town where I had been delivered a few years earlier, and we moved there. I went to fourth grade in Eldora.

By that age it had become more apparent that I soon would develop into a smart aleck. That, and me being a new kid in school, led to a brief playground skirmish. To call it a fight would inject much more drama into the scuffle than it deserves.

Some of us kids were playing marbles in the dust. Another kid walked up and out of the blue accused me of being scared to fight, or some such nonsense. I grabbed my marbles in both hands, jumped up, puffed out my hollow chest and glared at the accuser. Then I committed a tactical error. I shoved both of my hands into my pockets to secure my marbles. The kid recognized an opening and shoved me onto the seat of my pants in the dirt. By the time I could pull my hands out of my pockets and scramble to my feet my assailant had disappeared into the mob on the playground. Then the bell rang, ending recess.

Scott and I rode our bicycles a couple of miles out of Eldora to Pine Lake to fish or swim. The Iowa River, a much more intriguing fishing hole, flowed nearby, but we were forbidden to go there. Too dangerous. Moving water apparently posed more danger than still water. Parental admonition seldom persuaded Scott and me, especially when based on such flimsy reasoning. The river beckoned, mostly because we might catch a catfish. Catfish presented much more appealing prey than the sunfish and crappie that Pine Lake offered.

Dilemma of the Fish

On one of our outings to the forbidden river I became impaled on the horns of a dilemma. I caught a catfish! Actually, the fish caught itself. My line had snagged on something in the water. After struggling for a while to free the snag, I gave up, put down my pole and went to explore a nearby shallow stretch of the river. When the time came to go home, I picked up my pole and discovered a catfish had unsnagged my line. That foot-long channel catfish set my personal record biggest fish ever caught. It easily beat out the sunfish from Pine Lake and the chubs and bullheads that inhabited the creeks of my world.

Now the dilemma loomed before me. If I took home a catfish Dad would know Scott and I had been to the forbidden river. I rode my bicycle home with that catfish curled up in the front basket. Before long it had baked into a stiff, dry comma. Scott convinced me that the downside consequences would outweigh any pleasure I would enjoy from showing off my catch at home. I ditched the fish, eliminating all evidence that I had caught a bigger fish than Scott.

Near Drowning

I almost drowned in Pine Lake. Ironic. I never came close to drowning in the forbidden Iowa River. When we lived in Wellsburg, Mom and Dad had sent me to Grundy Center for swimming lessons. Kids from Wellsburg rode a school bus to Grundy during the early part of summer break. I had mixed feelings about those lessons. Riding the bus to the pool in Grundy was an adventure for a little kid who didn't ride a bus to school every day, but the frigid water in the pool turned me into a purple-lipped mass of goose bumps.

Those lessons did introduce me to the rudiments of swimming, though, and I got along pretty well in the pool. Then we moved to Eldora, and I discovered that swimming in a lake is different than swimming in a pool.

I joined swimming lessons at the beach. In order to pass to the next level, we had to swim out to the floating raft in the deeper water outside the beach ropes and back. It wasn't a long swim, and I was confident I could do it. Before I reached the raft a small wave crashed into my face. I gasped, swallowed, choked and lost momentum. Someone grabbed me and hauled me back to shallower water. That episode didn't plant a fear of water in me, but it did set back my progression through the ranks of swimming lessons.

Other Lessons

Fourth grade, around age nine, boys try what they perceive to be cool, slightly delinquent things they've seen bigger kids do. Mom Ford saw me spit once, at someone or just on the ground, I don't recall. She didn't approve of spitting for any reason. She sternly herded me out the back door of the house and made me spit twenty-five times in a row. After about five spits my saliva production couldn't keep up. Dry spitting requires effort. Try it, you won't like it. It'll make you stop spitting. Someone should make baseball players spit twenty-five times in a row before every game until they get the message about how ridiculous it looks. Who needs to spit that much?

Another time Mom heard me say a bad word of some kind and washed out my mouth with a bar of soap. Also unpleasant. After that I made sure Mom wasn't around if I felt the need to cuss. That episode probably has something to do with how public language used by many people today disturbs me to the core. It's an indication of the general decline in civility and values, and demonstrates that some people don't realize that their choice of words reflects upon their character. Or they don't care. Their mothers probably never washed out their mouths with a bar of Ivory. I can't claim that I don't swear – I play golf, after all – but I'm fully aware of those around me when I do cuss, and I try not to offend anyone.

Mom to the Rescue

Mom saved my bacon more than once. A small gang of us loitered near a house up the street throwing crab apples that had fallen out of a tree beside the street. I flung a missile at a utility pole down the street just as a car turned into the driveway beside the pole. My fruity grenade missed its intended target and splattered squarely on the roof of the car.

I should have followed my instincts as a delinquent and run off like the other guys. No, I expected the driver probably would ignore the assault or do no more than shout curses at me. If the driver did approach, I would simply explain that I had missed my intended target, the utility pole, and as luck would have it, he just happened to turn into that driveway at the wrong moment. We were both victims of circumstances.

That completely understandable explanation failed to satisfy the enraged man who climbed out of the car and stormed up the street. He grabbed me by the ear and demanded to know where I lived. He used my ear as a leash to drag me to our front door, upon which he knocked loudly. Mom answered the door and listened to a few words of his beef. I don't remember what the man told Mom, but he should have chosen his words more carefully. He apparently hinted during his tirade that it was a lousy parent who raised a child who would throw a rotten crab apple at a passing car. Mom bulled up and demanded that he let go of my ear and hit the road, NOW!

Dancing with Dad in the Basement

Mom always left it to Dad to meet out the physical punishment for the kids' transgressions. The crab apple incident fell into that category. That may have been the time Dad took me to the basement and broke a flamingo across my butt. Or that might have been after another corporal offense.

Dad put up with a lot, but sometimes he had to vent the accumulated frustrations of being a working adult with sons testing boundaries by swatting one us a few times. Scott and I each got walloped a time or two for the sins of the other, but it evened out. It depended on who was handy when the last straw hit Dad's load of life's disappointments. Actually, Dad spanked us less frequently than we deserved, probably because he felt the effort wouldn't produce the desired results. Or he was just too tired to deal with it.

This time, he marched me to the basement to administer punishment. All of the houses we lived in had basements where Dad retreated to work on his projects. I don't remember what the flamingoes were about, but Dad had cut a bunch of them out of flimsy particle board with his jigsaw. He probably planned to make a little extra money by selling yard ornaments. Dad could make stuff like that, but he lacked the business and marketing skills necessary to be successful. These days you're liable to see plastic pink flamingoes anywhere. They apparently have ornamental value that I don't recognize or appreciate. Perhaps they indicate membership in a secret organization, like the Masons.

Dad apparently thought one of his flamingoes would make a good paddle, having a thin neck he could grasp and a broad body for solid contact. It happened to be within reach at the time. The flamingo, fashioned of flimsy fiber board, broke on the first swat. Its body flew into a dusty corner. Dad and I dosey-doed a couple of rounds, me high-stepping to avoid blows from the flamingo neck and him doing little more than pulling on my shirt to keep my butt in range.

It didn't take more than one session to learn that if you started hollering and jumping around after the first smack, spankings didn't last long or amount to much. The humiliation always stung though, and lasted much longer than the slight pain. Getting spanked was embarrassing enough. The phony hollering and pretending to be hurt doubled the agony.

Sling Shots & Pea Shooters

Dad had a fair collection of hand tools and a few power tools in the basement. His father, Fred Ford, could make cabinets and other items of furniture out of wood. Dad probably absorbed some of his craftsmanship from his father. I can hammer nails and cut boards but never grew enough patience to be a wood worker.

That's the same lack that steered me toward journalism rather than more long forms of writing. Writing comes easily, but lacking patience, literature has no appeal to me, other than for reading. During my career, news stories I wrote in a few minutes and moved on, instant gratification. Also, deadlines overcome inertia. Deadlines eliminate prolonged procrastination. I require deadlines. Writing this memoir has been difficult. It's taking too long, and other than certain death, and who knows when that will happen, or the possibility of dementia, no deadline prods me along.

The months we lived in Eldora, many of the kids played marbles before and after school and during recess. We carried our little marble bags around with us. Depending upon how well you flipped your shooter each day, your bag grew fatter or thinner.

I also got into shooting slingshots and pea shooters. To make pea shooters, we cut short sections out of the aluminum tubes of old television antennas we found in trash heaps. A bag of small dried beans or peas cost a quarter or less. You could cram a handful of beans into your mouth and blast them through your pea shooter like a machine gun. One time I bumped the muzzle of my pea shooter on something and the breech end cut the roof of my mouth. That's a memory my brain should have repressed. It still makes me wince.

First Prize

I won the first prize of my life in Eldora. It wasn't a first-place prize, just a prize, my first. The Parent-Teacher Association held a school carnival with makeshift games, a bake sale and raffle drawings. After I had played the games and entered my name in the raffles my interest lagged and I walked home. Someone called our house a little while later and said my name had been drawn at the school carnival. I walked back to the school and claimed my prize, a diaper bag.

One day while on the sidewalk near home, I spied a bumble bee in the middle of the street wrestling with some other critter or object. I picked up a wooden toy letter block that happened to be just there and casually tossed it in a high arc in the direction of the bee. One corner of the block struck point perfect right on the bee, which never knew what hit it. I've never had a hole-in-one in fifty years of playing golf, but I hit that bee with the corner of a little wooden block from fifteen feet, first try. Why does a person remember silly little things like that?

Bait Goes Bad

We lived on the edge of Eldora, near the railroad tracks. Scott and I seined crawdads from a murky creek in a pasture a half mile from our house. No more than a foot or two wide in most spots, the creek teemed with crayfish, just about the best bait going for the catfish we planned to catch out of the Iowa River. We dumped a squirming mass of crawdads into a wash tub behind our garage and promptly forgot about them. After a couple of hours all the crayfish were dead and turned orange. By the next day the whole yard stunk.

A couple of boys near Scott's and my ages lived in a two-room shack by the railroad tracks a quarter mile from our house. My family never had much beyond what it took to get by, but this family had virtually nothing. A five-gallon bucket just inside the front door served as a toilet. I was in the hovel only once. I don't recall seeing a bathtub or shower. A man who I presumed was the father, a tiny rack of a human being dressed in filth, sat on the bucket smoking and coughing. That scene branded my brain where memories accumulate. Sixty years later, in obscure fringe pockets of my current city, Columbia, Missouri, people live in sleeping bags, without buckets.

Distant Developments

Around this time, unknown to me, my future family – the Stewarts in Missouri – began to grow. My mother, Donna, gave birth to my half-sister Jacqueline (Jackie) Sue on December 18, 1956. I was eight. Jackie's sister, my half-sister Valerie Joye, came along about two years later, on September 14, 1958.

It would be six years before I would meet these two sisters and eight years before I moved in with the Stewart family in Gladstone.

CHAPTER 4

RETURN TO GRUNDY CENTER

The Ford family didn't live in Eldora long enough, barely a year, for me to develop any long-lasting connections. Dad had transitioned from an auto mechanic to a body-and-fender man. He banged out dents, patched rusted rocker panels and painted over his repairs. Bosses rubbed Dad wrong, so he tried out a new one regularly. We moved back to Grundy Center in the latter half of the 1950s. This time we lived there from my fifth-grade year until the summer of 1964, after my sophomore year in high school.

Dad moved us into an old brick two-story house behind Vogt's ice cream shop, which was catty-corner from the Courthouse. We lived there only briefly, six months at most. A gas station sat on the corner across from Vogt's, and the Spokesman Press building sat across the street from our house. Mom told us an old lady lived in the house before us. She had died. Mom claimed she saw the ghost of an old lady in the house.

Mom liked spooks and scary stuff. While we were living in Wellsburg, before Dad and LaVelle got married, they went to a movie at the theater in Grundy. Scott and I, in the three- and four-year-old range, went along. The movie villain injected a potion into another man and turned him into an ape that terrorized people at night. It terrorized me at night for several years. Scary movies, ghosts and other eeriness entertained Mom. When a funeral procession would pass, she delighted in singing a ditty that began

"Did you ever think when the hearse went by that you might be the next to die?" No lullabies for her.

Basement Bathing

The old lady of our house apparently had bad memories of the Great Depression of the 1930s and the material shortages during World War II. When we moved into the house several dozen wilted rolls of toilet paper reached in forlorn stacks from the toilet tank toward the bathroom ceiling.

We took baths in a washtub in the basement, which had a dirt floor. Because hot water had to be toted from the kitchen to the washtub, more than one of us washed in the same water. If you weren't first, and I never was, you bathed in your own dirt plus the dirt of all those who had gone before. Those baths made me itch all over and certainly left me no cleaner than before the bath. I felt the old lady's ghost spying on me in the tub.

We lived in that house when my youngest Ford sibling, half-sister Karin, was born on November 29, 1957.

I had my tenth birthday while we lived there. I remember that only because it was Easter Sunday 1958. A thunderstorm rumbled through town early that day, after which the sun broke through, providing me with a balmy birthday. Another of my birthdays fell on Easter in 1969 while I was suffering through electronics training at Millington Naval Air Station just north of Memphis, Tennessee. I don't remember that birthday being on Easter, but it comes back later in this story. It was my twenty-first.

Coal Down Below

Dad soon found a larger house in Grundy Center. It had a detached garage, a larger basement with a concrete floor, and enough bedrooms upstairs for all five of us kids and a guest, in the event we ever had one. Scott and I shared, as usual. Separate bedrooms for Scott and I seemed a waste of a room, and it never occurred to either of us to question the arrangement. Our twin beds fit easily into our new bedroom.

The basement housed a massive coal-burning furnace, a small storeroom for canned vegetables, a coal room to store the fuel for the furnace, and a shop area that held Dad's wood lathe, table saw, drill and other tools. Scott and I had the chore of keeping the furnace coal hopper filled. Before winter came a truck backed up to a rear corner of the house and poured chunked coal into the coal room through an opening in the house's foundation. Each morning before school one of us shoveled coal into the hopper, which fed the constantly burning fire in the massive furnace. Heat rose of its own will through ducts, most of it captured by the rooms on the lower level of the house. Us kids, in the upstairs bedrooms, wore lots of clothes, including heavy socks, to bed in the winter. I learned to fill a rubber hot water bottle and put it between my sheets a few minutes before going to bed.

Dad cut and turned wood in the basement, producing picture frames, lamps and sawdust. I piddled on small projects. For a Scout or school shop project I crafted a chess board, complete with shellacked squares of contrasting colors. I swept Dad's and my sawdust into a dustpan, opened the furnace door and pitched the load into the mound of glowing coal embers. The sawdust exploded like a Fourth of July rocket. Cool. That became one of my occasional winter pastimes.

Dad always planted a garden somewhere in town each spring. He tortured Scott and me with weeding and the harvest. To this day, a bowl of green beans on the table evokes bad memories of getting all sweaty and itchy in a garden. Fresh tomatoes were my favorite. I kept a close eye out for those big black and yellow spiders that always lurked among the ripe tomatoes.

Mom canned the vegetables. She once sent me down to the cellar to get a jar of green beans or corn from the storeroom. When I reached for the light switch on the door frame of the storeroom a bolt of pure pain shot through my hand and tried to jerk my arm out of its socket. That dim, dusty basement, spooky enough without high-voltage booby traps, grew more menacing. Also, my appetite for canned vegetables waned.

Weekly Washup

At our house, until we got into junior high and started showering regularly because of sports and developing social awareness, the kids got their weekly baths on Saturday night. That habit probably developed with the thought of having clean kids if they happen to go to church the next morning. Also, after a Saturday of running amok, kids needed a rinsing.

The Methodist Church was two blocks away, so that's where the kids were sent. Mom and Dad never attended church that I recall, not even on Easter or Christmas. After a season of Vacation Bible School and Sunday church, I got into the routine of detouring to a gas station on main street and hanging out for an hour before going home to change into my regular clothes.

Going to Work

Scott turned over part of his paper route to me late in the Fifties. The prospect of making a couple of bucks a week appealed to me. Virtually every morning for the next three years I delivered *The Des Moines Register* to about thirty homes in the southeast quadrant of Grundy Center. Thirty doesn't sound like a lot of papers to deliver, and it isn't if the houses are clustered nicely. These weren't. It would have taken a committee of urban planners a couple of meetings to figure out how to scatter thirty houses farther apart from each other in that section of town.

The paper route was my first job with the potential for outside income. Note that word "potential." Newspaper carriers work on a slim profit margin. Each week the newspaper company sent me a bill for the papers I had delivered that week. The company had an account at a local bank. Before the bank closed at noon on Saturday, I had to deposit my collections.

After delivering the Saturday morning papers, I made another circuit of my route, knocking on the front door of each of my customers to collect for that week's papers, 35 cents for the daily paper, 55 cents for the daily plus Sunday. I favored my 55-cent customers who got the paper every day. They paid more and I didn't have to remember if they got a paper each day. Sunday-only customers were a pain. A few of my customers didn't answer my knocks, so collections always fell a dollar or two shy of the bill from the newspaper. After repeated visits to the delinquent customers, I collected another dollar or two to add to next week's bank deposit.

The publisher in Des Moines never sent a collection agent to threaten to fire me if I didn't square my account each week. But a rep from the paper did appear every couple of months to deliver a pep talk on the Courthouse square to the small crew of local carriers. He offered cool prizes like a pocket knife or flashlight for signing up new customers. I lacked sales skills, so my route didn't expand much. The rare new customer I signed up always seemed to fall into that group that didn't answer my knocks on collection day.

Winter Pain

When snow and ice covered the ground, I had to walk my route. Dad sometimes drove me around on Sunday mornings when the temperature plummeted to below zero. Deep snow prevented bicycling, and the heavy Sunday edition required at least two trips to the post office if I had to walk. Dad smoked, a lot. Riding around in that haze with the windows closed against the cold upset my stomach and made me dizzy.

One winter the temperature fell to thirty below zero for several straight nights. My hands and feet nearly froze every morning as I walked my route. With fingers beyond feeling, I struggled to get my coat and boots off after staggering into the house. Severe pain shot through my fingers and toes for several minutes as they warmed slowly. I cried sometimes before the pain subsided enough for me to take off my boots, eat a bowl of Rice Krispies and walk to school.

Installment Bicycle

Around this time, I got a lesson in buying something on credit and making payments. Dad and Mom knew that I desperately wanted to get a new bicycle for my birthday. I had a mutt of a bike, pieced together, rattley and hard to peddle up hills. A bicycle made delivering my papers each morning a much faster operation, at least when snow didn't make riding impossible. Just getting to the post office to pick up my papers went from a ten-minute walk to a three-minute ride.

On the day of my birthday, I couldn't wait to see what kind of bicycle I'd get. I wanted one of those sleek "English" models with skinny tires and three gears that you changed by flicking a small lever on the handle bar.

What I got was an envelope with a $5 check inside. My folks explained that with that money I could make a down payment on the bicycle I wanted at the Western Auto store on main street. After a couple of days recovering from the crushing disappointment, I went to the hardware store. Dad must have told the store owner that he would back me up, payment-wise, because I left the store with a brand-new, skinny-tired, three-speed English bicycle. The deal: $5 down and $1 a week until paid off. Unfortunately, English bikes weren't built for delivering newspapers. The payments lasted longer than the bicycle.

The Music Died

I picked up my bundle of papers, marked Route 110, from the dock behind the post office down by the city power plant a block past main street. A front-page story early in February 1959 reported that rock-and-roll singer Buddy Holly (Peggy Sue) died in a plane crash in northern Iowa along with

Ritchie Valens (La Bamba) and J.P. "The Big Bopper" Richardson (Chantilly Lace). They had just finished a gig at the Surf Ballroom in Clear Lake, Iowa, 87 miles from Grundy.

Here's a trivia question that I'm sorry to say I didn't know the answer to in a minor local fundraiser in 2018: "What was the name of the plane that crashed with Buddy Holly aboard?" Singer/songwriter Don McClean's 1971 hit anthem "American Pie" begins with an obscure reference to the crash, calling it "the day the music died." American Pie – the name of the airplane. Dope slap. Nobody on my trivia team knew the plane even had a name. The music died a short time before I started paying attention to the rock-and-roll hits of the day.

One stormy morning when I was kneeling on the post office dock stuffing my papers into my delivery bag, a bolt of lightning struck the power plant just across the parking lot. The lightning cleaved the early-morning darkness with a blinding canon shot that I swear lifted me off the dock. The jolt caused no permanent damage at the power plant, but I was still shaking when I got home after delivering my papers.

Treetop Outpost

Our house was on a corner two blocks away from the house we had lived in before we moved to Eldora. Dad's parents, Grandpa and Grandma Ford, Fred and Cora (Grandpa called her Dollie) lived a block and a half west on our street. Our house had a fine front porch that we seldom used, a garage out back and a loosely covered cistern in the side yard that earlier inhabitants had used to store rainwater.

A boy my age and his older sister lived in a house on one of the other corners of the intersection. In the corner of their yard, between the sidewalk and the street, rose a spectacular tree. I never paid any attention to what kind of tree it was, and it's been gone for many years. The tree's numerous, evenly spaced horizontal branches made for easy climbing. Carvings in the bark, mostly hearts with initials in them, indicated that many kids in town knew about the tree and had explored its grandeur. A few of the carvings contained my initials along with those of girls I had secret crushes on. I often climbed to the very top of that tree and gazed out over the expanse of Grundy County.

Across another street lived a boy Scott's age. We rarely saw him or his parents. They just never seemed to leave their house. One summer a swarm of honey bees took up residence in a front corner eave of their house. I sat down in their front yard and put my hands down behind my back. My left hand smothered a bee that I didn't see. It sent me howling home. A beekeeper came and removed the hive.

I never knew who lived in the house directly through the intersection, but it had a huge lilac bush out front.

Chicken Butchers

A grotesquely fat man and his equally obese wife lived in the house next to the people with the bees. We didn't often see an obese person back then. Every class in school had at least one chubby kid, who took a lot of teasing because of it, but obesity was as rare as Christmas. Our fat neighbors butchered chickens for a living. I went over and watched them a few times. They didn't seem to mind a nosy kid or two hanging around watching them chop the heads off and eviscerating whole flocks of fowl. Semi trucks delivered to the couple's driveway flatbed trailers stacked high with squat wooden-and-wire cages full of chickens. Neighborhood kids knew where to find entertainment any time one of those trailers appeared.

Without leaving their seats except to carry in the next cage of chickens, the couple processed the birds in a small room attached to a back corner of their house. After lopping off the chickens' heads, they stuck the birds feet-up in large funnels attached in a row along a wall. A decapitated chicken exhibits a peculiar behavior. It runs. If it's on the ground it will flap its wings and flop around. Sticking the headless birds neck down into the funnels held them in place until their legs stopped flailing.

After the birds stopped running in air, the corpses went into a steaming pot of water to loosen the feathers. A gadget with spinning rubber fingers plucked the feathers before the butchers removed the innards.

The couple chopped, plucked and sliced their way through a trailer-load of chickens in a couple of days.

Tree Tag

The kid we seldom saw lived across the street from our house and next door to the chicken pickers. In the two houses on the opposite side of the butchers lived boys my age. We played tag among the branches of a maple tree in the yard of the house on the corner. If the kid who was "it" pursued you onto a limb of the tree, you could fall or jump to another branch to escape. We played catch up there, too, with a football. If you made a poor throw, you had to climb down and retrieve the ball. If you fumbled a catch, you had to get the ball. It never occurred to me to tell the high school football coach to send his quarterbacks and receivers up a tree. If you're playing catch in a tree, you pay attention, and not just to the ball.

Part of this tree, which turned a spectacular scarlet/orange in the fall, hung over a street. One time a car came along while we were up in the tree playing catch. I thought it would be funny to drop the ball on the car, so I did. The driver didn't believe my excuse that we were playing catch, and I just missed the ball at the wrong time. He didn't think it was funny either. What could he do? I was up a tree. On the other hand, I was up a tree. All he had to do was wait.

That turned out to be not as funny as I thought it would be. It took several years for it to sink in that something that appears worth doing on the front side can have an unpleasant back side. It's better to consider possible outcomes before doing a deed. Failing that, one needs to establish an escape route or a plausible alibi, just in case. If you get really good at creating plausible deniability, you can become a politician. Earlier events in my life hinted at this lesson about thinking ahead, but it would be several more years before it sank in.

Bat Hunt

A bat got into our house one day. Mom nearly expired, on account. She believed that a bird in the house, ignoring the fact that a bat is a mammal, not a bird, meant someone in the family was going to die. Whoever planted that idea in her youthful brain had committed child abuse, just like when she and Dad took Scott and me to the gorilla movie. The way Mom carried on she must have believed the bat had come for her. Most probably she just used the story to scare us kids.

I located a weapon – a slat from a snow fence – and crept upstairs, where the creature lurked. Upstairs had a loop from the hallway where Scott and I wrestled, through the bathroom and two bedrooms back to the hallway. I hadn't been up there a minute and was standing in my sister Candy's bedroom when the bat swooped around a corner, right toward me. With both hands on the stick I swung it down from over my head and smacked the bat to the floor. It slid under Candy's bed, dead.

Whether killing the bat lifted the curse, I don't recall, but none of us died right then.

Scaling the Standpipe

Across the street from the elementary school, on the highest spot in town, a water tower rose into the sky. We called it the standpipe because that's basically what it was, a huge pipe standing on end. A narrow steel ladder attached to the side of the standpipe rose to the top. Like other delinquents had done, I climbed the standpipe one night. If you had never climbed the standpipe, you carried no weight among the rowdy.

Dad was a member of Grundy Center's volunteer fire department. Whenever the fire alarm sounded, any of the available volunteers jumped into their cars and raced to the fire station. The fire alarm didn't necessarily mean something was on fire. The volunteers responded to emergencies of all kinds, even the routine variety.

After lying on top of the standpipe and looking down, only the thought of the volunteer fire department coming to rescue me got me back on the ladder for the climb down. Never again did an urge to climb a water tower overpower my memory of lying on my belly on top of that standpipe peering into the abyss. Along about this time I began to realize that sometimes second thoughts, which are warnings after all, should overrule initial impulses.

CHAPTER 5

ENTER THE ATHLETE

$\int$ cott and I played little league baseball for a few weeks during summer. I played first base because every kid had to play somewhere, and I had no arm for the outfield. One summer my team won the league championship. We had a pitcher whose fastball scared the daylights out of all the other kids. Denny also had a great pick-off move, disguised by a balk, in case he walked someone. Our umpires didn't recognize balks.

Grandpa Ford showed up in the rickety ballfield bleacher one day, a total surprise to me. Our parents, and certainly our grandparents, never took much notice of anything any of us kids did, in school or out. Many parents were like that, especially during summer baseball when they were working, so we didn't feel neglected.

My baseball skills rose to the level of my basketball skills and no higher. Batting exposed a particular weakness. If I ever did connect with a pitch, the ball popped up feebly or limped out to the pitcher, who threw me out. On the day Grandpa Ford showed up, we must have faced a particularly poor pitcher. My first time up, I laced a drive down the line into right field for a triple. On my next at bat, the right fielder paid closer attention. I smacked another shot down the line; he held me to a double.

Except for the opponent's pitcher and right fielder, I was the most surprised person at the ball park. Grandpa Ford probably thought I would take over for Mickey Mantle in a few years. Maybe Grandpa came to the ball park to watch me play because he knew he was dying, which he did not many months after the only two-hit baseball game of my Little League career.

Early Retirement

My baseball career ended when I tried out for the high school team. Early in the season the team practiced in the school gym because of the late-winter cold and mud on the ball field. We warmed up by playing catch. The problem had never manifested outdoors, but in the gym, I had trouble seeing the ball clearly as it approached my nose. That made me uneasy, as you might imagine. I seemed destined to suffer a broken nose or black eye if this continued. Knowing that the Spartans could get along without any contribution from me, I quit the team.

It occurred to me that an eye exam might be in order. The man who ran the little storefront optometry shop on main street confirmed that, yes, I was near-sighted. He soon had me fixed up with my first pair of glasses. The exam and glasses cost $15. I made payments. On my walk home from the optical shop, individual blades of grass and leaves in the trees popped out at me, a revelation. Lawns and trees had just been masses of green before that.

Gridiron Glory

Scott was two grades ahead of me in school. We didn't typically hang together unless none of our usual co-conspirators were handy. Scott and his friends went out for all of the sports they could in school, but mainly football. Some wrestled, ran track, played baseball and basketball. Junior high sports only whetted my appetite for the real thing. I couldn't wait to get to high school football and wrestling.

When I was in eighth grade, my football team went undefeated, 4-0. I played end on offense and defense. We outscored our opponents 99-0 in those four games. We didn't throw many passes. About all I did on offense was get in the way of a defender. Once in a while the quarterback would throw a pass over my head or into the dirt behind me. My pulse picked up on defense. For some reason, none of the offensive lines we played against could figure out how to block me. I always lined up outside the widest player on the offensive line. That often gave me a free shot at the ball carrier. If I didn't get him, I slowed him down until the heavies in the line smothered him. Once after I'd made an easy tackle for a loss, I heard one of the opposing players, returning to his huddle, whine, "Who's supposed to be blocking 76?" That was me, number 76.

A bunch of the kids around my age played football in yards around town. We all had visions of glory ahead when our turn came to play school ball. One time all of us got together on the junior high football field and played a real game. I learned while making a tackle in that game that "seeing stars" is a real thing. Games against friends in the yard and scrimmages during school practices banged me up more than any real football game I ever played in.

Suiting Up

A couple of the kids had helmets, but most of us had no gear beyond footballs. I determined to outfit myself. With a pair of long underwear, top and bottom, and a bunch of newspaper, I figured I could sew up a passable football uniform. Grandma Ford had all the sewing equipment, needle and thread. I set to work at her house.

I sewed cloth pockets inside the underwear at appropriate places for shoulder, thigh and knee pads. Into these pockets I stuffed wadded up newspapers. My excitement grew as the project neared completion. Needle work finished, I rushed into the bathroom to change into my football uniform.

Flaws in my design revealed themselves. Imagine a skinny kid in tight long underwear with bulging lumps deforming his shoulders and legs. A humorous image if you've got any imagination. I was crushed, and would have cried if I hadn't looked so ridiculous. My uniform never saw the out-of-doors, let alone a front-yard football field.

A junior high hurdle-relay team I ran with won a first-place trophy at a large track meet in Cedar Falls. The five-inch tall prize we received claimed a spot in the junior high school trophy case, which still displayed years of hardware accumulated when the building housed the high school grades. My relay team's plastic gold cup looked toy-like among those tarnished prizes of past glory.

Once during an individual event at a track meet behind the school, a hurdle snagged my knee and dumped me on my back in the cinders. I got up and limped over the finish line. The couple of dozen spectators in the bleachers applauded my last-place effort.

Hitting the Mat

The high school wrestling team, including my brother Scott, practiced in the gym of the elementary school, up the sledding hill from the junior high building. The wrestlers had to walk or drive a few blocks from the high school that had opened in the 1950s. I often watched the wrestlers practice after school.

Basketball and wrestling seasons ran at the same time during winter. My efforts to play basketball in junior high revealed a significant lack of talent for the game, and it didn't call to me loudly enough to inspire me to get better. Attempting basketball in high school didn't even cross my mind.

The upstairs level of our house, where the kids' bedrooms were, had a spacious hallway at the top of the stairs. Scott and I spread sleeping bags on the floor and wrestled. He always won, but not without a fight.

The elementary school where Scott and I attended in our earlier stay in Grundy Center had three levels. The coach made the wrestlers run up and down the stairs. Years later the coach wrote a brief poetic essay about those steps and the part they played in the wrestling team's training. He printed the essay on a photo of the stairs and presented framed copies to his wrestlers. I had left Grundy long before the coach produced those mementoes. Scott gave me a copy.

I compiled a decent record wrestling on the junior varsity team in my freshman and sophomore years. Most of the kids I wrestled weren't as good as my brother. The coach once split the JV team for meets in two different places on the same night. The bunch he put me in went to Eldora to wrestle boys in reform school there. I pinned my opponent in the first period of the match after he nearly scored a takedown. The reform school boys wrestled well for kids with little coaching.

A couple of times I lost matches to kids that I should have beaten easily. Those losses irritated me. They also exhausted me beyond the usual fast physical recovery of a teen-ager. It took some of those losses for me to learn that high school kids need to eat and sleep well if they expect to win. If eating well means getting your fill, the Ford family seldom ate well. A typical meal consisted of a tuna casserole or a package of wieners baked in a dish of beans. A family of seven leaves no leftovers.

I listened to a rock music station out of Waterloo on a cheap little transistor radio while I walked to the high school for wrestling meets and football games. If the 1963 hit "Dominique" by The Singing Nun came on during the walk, I gained confidence that I'd win my match that night. I didn't understand the French lyrics, but the melody pumped me up. Now when I watch a pregame program on television and some of the players are shown with their headphones on and heads bobbing, I know what they're doing.

Twice during high school sports practices, once wrestling and the other time football, I suffered severely sprained ankles. Neither time did I get any medical attention beyond the coach taping the ankle. Other than taping, coaches had little time or expertise in dealing with injuries, especially to those suffered by second-stringers. After both sprains, I hobbled around slowly for a couple of weeks until the pain went away.

Teaming Up

Scott and I got to play high school football together for two years. Actually, the only together part occurred on the practice field. He played on the varsity, I played junior varsity. During scrimmages, varsity on offense, JV on defense, my tackling technique involved jumping on the ball carrier's back and riding him until help arrived.

The Spartans went undefeated in the 1962 season, Scott's junior and my freshman year. A 6-6 tie in the Homecoming game blemished the record. Games at that time still were being played on the field behind what had become the junior high school. The school invited all the members of the 1962 team back for a commemoration on the 25h anniversary of that season. Scott and I attended. The school put on a program with speeches and entertainment in the auditorium and recognized the players from the 1962 team during that week's football game.

The new football field at the high school opened for play in the fall of 1963, when I was a sophomore and Scott was a senior. The junior varsity played the first game on the field. My best friend threw a pass to me in the right flat. I caught the ball and tippy-toed through a mud puddle in the endzone for the first touchdown on the new field. We got our tails whipped in that game. The better players in my class were assigned to the varsity, so they couldn't play with the junior varsity. The squad that had gone 4-0 in junior high didn't compete as ferociously as a high school junior varsity team.

The varsity, after its undefeated record the previous season, went 4-4. It did win the Homecoming game, a measure of redemption for tying that game a year earlier.

Chapter 6

Life Gets More Serious

Grandpa and Grandma Ford's house didn't have running water, which I thought interesting. They lived right in town! A pump in a sink in a corner of the kitchen brought up rainwater from a cistern. They heated pots of water on the stove and poured them into the tub in the bathroom whenever they decided to take baths.

Grandpa Ford worked at the city power plant. He chain smoked. He lit his next cigarette with the glowing butt of the one between his fingers. An ash tray sat on the edge of the bathtub beside the toilet. It always contained numerous butts and long strands of cigarette ash. Smoking killed Grandpa Ford. I know that because I read his death certificate that had been left on top of a curio cabinet in their dining room. Dad and Scott went to the hospital to visit Grandpa just before he died. They discouraged me from going along with them. When they got home, Scott said he wished he hadn't gone.

Grandpa Ford was 76 years old when he died on December 13, 1963. I was 15. He's buried in the cemetery at Grundy Center. Grandma Ford, Cora (Grandpa called her Dollie), went to live with one of Dad's sisters in Michigan sometime after Grandpa Ford died. She passed away there on October 26, 1971, age 83.

Grandpa and Grandma Ford, perhaps at a wedding anniversary observance. The people in back may have been Grandpa Ford's siblings, nobody identified them on the photograph. Judging by their expressions, they appear to be cut from the same somber cloth.

Grandma Sitting

Scott and I mowed grass and shoveled snow for Grandpa and Grandma Ford. He sometimes paid us for the work we did, but he grumbled about it. He expressed his displeasure after I shoveled a heavy load of deep snow off his front walk one time. "It looks like a drunk sailor did that," he growled. I never in my life saw my Grandpa Ford smile. Maybe he did when he witnessed my triple and double on the baseball field. I hope so.

After Grandpa Ford died, Scott and I took turns sleeping at his house to look after Grandma. We slept in a bed upstairs with a chamber pot under it. On one of my nights I discovered that Grandma had locked the front and back doors. I climbed onto the roof of the front porch, found a window that wasn't locked, crawled in and went to bed.

Classmate's Funeral

Nobody in my family listened to radio much. I started listening in the 1960s, when you could buy a pocket transistor radio that ran on batteries for $10. Then you could carry music with you.

Scott and I listened briefly early in the mornings before getting out of bed and at night before going to sleep. The radio sat on a little table between our twin beds. That radio told us one Sunday morning that a kid in my freshman class had been killed in a car crash the night before. I know Scott was awake, too, but we laid in stunned silence, not wanting to believe what we'd heard. For some reason we couldn't even look at one another.

The boy wasn't a close friend, in fact he ran with that small group of kids considered "hoods" because he drove a car when he was a freshman, rolled a pack of cigarettes in the sleeve of his T-shirt and sported a James Dean haircut and attitude. Grundy Center isn't large, at that time about 2,500 people. The boy lived in a much smaller town nearby. Virtually everybody knew him or his family. He had sped around a curve right beside his yard. His car rolled and his neck broke.

Some of my friends and I went to the funeral home to view our classmate in his casket. The next day, school let out so everyone who wanted to could attend the funeral. Many did. The church was full.

Commies Scare Mom

Another banner headline on my bundled papers, this one from early May 1960, announced that an American U2 spy plane had been shot down over Russia. The incident resulted in one of the most frigid periods of the Cold War. President Dwight Eisenhower's administration had to work out a trade, our pilot Gary Powers in exchange for a Russian spy in United States' custody. That was one of the final acts of Ike's presidency. John Kennedy defeated Richard Nixon in the 1960 election in November and would soon be inaugurated to succeed Eisenhower.

An international news story like the U2 shoot-down normally wouldn't attract the attention of a twelve-year-old. But even in central Iowa, people feared that the tension between the Soviet Union and the United States could at any time turn from cold to hot. The McCarthy hearings in the Senate in the 1950s had almost dispelled the paranoia that Russian spies lurked all over the country, but the Cuban Missile Crisis loomed just ahead, reprising the fear.

People in the Midwest had good reason to fear. The U.S. Strategic Air Command (SAC), which perpetually patrolled the Earth's sky, had headquarters in eastern Nebraska. Until 25 years ago, scattered around the countryside in the upper Midwest were underground silos that held intercontinental ballistic missiles. After the heat of the Cold War cooled, those missiles were removed and the silos were destroyed late in the 20th Century. An enemy launching missiles against the U.S. almost certainly would have targeted SAC command and those missile silos in the opening volley. If not the bullseye for a missile barrage, the upper Midwest wasn't far from it.

Dad didn't pay much attention to world affairs. He was busy earning enough to pay rent and buy groceries. Mom, on the other hand, stayed home, where her memories of World War II, which had ended just fifteen years earlier, stoked her fear of a Communist invasion or a nuclear war.

The collaboration of the Unites States with the other Allied nations, including Russia, had led to the defeat of Adolph Hitler and the Nazis by forcing the Germans to fight on two fronts in World War II. Everyone knew that cooperation would end when the war did. Democracies had partnered with Communist Russia to defeat a common enemy, not to forge a lasting friendship.

The Cuban Missile Crisis, which put the entire developed world on edge in October 1962, stoked Mom's fears. She expected bombs to rain down on us at any moment. After a couple of weeks of world tension, U.S. and Soviet officials worked out a deal to cool down the Cuban crisis.

Stiffed

After I quit my paper route, when I was 14, I got a job at a restaurant on main street. It had a half dozen booths along one wall and three or four tables in the middle of the floor. On weekends I worked fourteen or more hours to complete a twelve-hour shift. The shift covered the hours the restaurant was open. It didn't cover the hours before opening when I helped prepare, or the hours after closing when I helped clean up. My wage – 80 cents an hour – came to $9.60 for the round-the-clock shift. Throw in the $0.00 I got for the extra hours of work, and my wage came up shy of 70 cents an hour.

One night my turn came up to stay with Grandma Ford. After my shift at the restaurant, I walked to Grandma's house and went to bed. The piercing pain in my feet prevented sleep. Tears tickled my cheeks as they trickled into my ears. (Restaurant servers labor near the bottom of the pay scale. I always tip heavily for good service.)

Some of the high school kids came into the restaurant for burgers and fries. One of my friends always dropped a coin in the jukebox by the front door and punched the letter and number on the music menu for The Beatles' "I Saw Her Standing There." The song added pep to my step.

A stunning weather event occurred during the brief time I worked at the restaurant. I stood behind the high school and watched as a boiling black mass approached from the west. A solid wall of dust two hundred feet high roared through town. The dirt storm left a layer of silt over everything. Grit had blown through invisible gaps around doors and windows.

That afternoon I worked frantically in the dining room of the restaurant to get it clean enough to serve customers. The few who came in that evening had to put up with a little dirt, but they probably were there only because their own kitchens were filthy.

One day soon after that a sign taped to the restaurant door greeted me as I arrived for work. The restaurant had been closed down. The owner had left town, I learned later. He owed me $30. I don't know how many bills the man skipped out on, but the way I figured it, he stiffed me for at least 40 hours of work.

Early Politics

Those early years of my life, in Wellsburg, Eldora and Grundy Center, occurred in the decade of the 1950s into the 60s. The Korean War spanned four of those years, from late spring 1950 to summer 1953. Harry Truman was the president until early 1953, but I don't remember anything about him or the Korean War. Dwight Eisenhower, the Allied commander and hero of World War II, won the presidency in November 1952 and was inaugurated early in 1953. "Ike" played a lot of golf, that's what I remember about his time in the White House.

Eisenhower served until the election of John Kennedy in November 1960. Kennedy and his opponent, Richard Nixon, held the first televised presidential candidate debates. Many historians say Kennedy eked out his narrow victory in the election because he looked better on television than Nixon, who sweated under the hot television lighting in the first of four debates. In the grainy picture on our television, neither of them looked sweaty to me.

I could not vote, of course, but it was around this time that my political ideology began to form. For a reason unknown to me, it sprouted with a leftward tilt and has maintained that attitude. Democrats seemed to care more about working people, and I had been surrounded by them my entire life. My memories of going to bed and to school hungry on many occasions no doubt contributed to my political leaning. Liberals seemed to be more concerned about things like that than conservatives.

Chapter 7

Mournful Thanksgiving

Just before noon on Friday, November 22, 1963, I was in sophomore study hall at Grundy Center High School. With the Thanksgiving break just days away, high spirits prevailed. A classmate, Curtis, had left our table in the library and gone to the bathroom.

Curtis and I, being nearly the same size, squared off most days at wrestling practice after school. We were junior varsity. Many years later, when I returned to Grundy Center for the thirtieth reunion of the class of 1966, I saw in a downtown store window a display with black ribbons and photographs of several classmates who had died. A photo of Curtis was among them. "How did Curtis die?" I asked a classmate. "He ran his motorcycle into the side of a moving train."

Another classmate whose picture hung in the window crashed an airplane while taking flying lessons. He had been the almost unstoppable fullback on my eighth-grade football team that went undefeated. A third classmate, whose family got its morning *Des Moines Register* from me for three years, died in a car accident.

Curtis returned to study hall. "The President was shot," he said. I thought that a strange thing for him to say. A murmur spread among the students. Then a teacher came into the room and got everyone's attention. "President Kennedy has been shot," the teacher said. Gasps and cries erupted all around. High school students typically didn't pay much attention to national politics, but among young people John Kennedy was a popular president, a handsome 46-year-old compared to previous presidents. Something of a rock star with a beautiful wife and young children.

Because of the televised debates before his election, even with fuzzy black-and-white television images, virtually everyone knew what John Kennedy looked and sounded like. When the teacher told us the president had been shot, Kennedy's condition was unknown. Everyone in the school building, some of them weeping, gathered in the halls. Crowds formed under the television monitors mounted at intervals near the ceiling above the rows of lockers. I had never paid much attention to those monitors until then. CBS newsman Walter Cronkite narrated the live video from Dallas, Texas, where the shooting occurred. Then a live shot showed Cronkite in the studio. "President Kennedy died at 1 p.m.," he said.

The school principal cancelled classes for the rest of the day. Dazed students streamed out of the building and went home to face a somber weekend. The assassination story had just begun.

Drama on TV

I spent many hours lying on the floor in our living room watching the grainy, live coverage of the drama in Dallas and then in Washington, D.C. I watched Lee Harvey Oswald, the 24-year-old suspect, being taken into the police station in Dallas. I watched a police officer hold up the rifle they believed Oswald used to shoot the president. Two days after the assassination, when the suspect was being transferred to another jail, I watched on live television as Dallas nightclub owner Jack Ruby stepped out of a crowd of cops and gunned down Oswald in the basement of the Dallas Police Department.

Ruby, a police department gadfly, had enjoyed rubbing elbows with local cops. He sometimes took doughnuts or sandwiches to police headquarters.

The cops knew him, so seeing him there when Oswald was being transferred raised no concerns. A few years later, Jack Ruby died in prison of lung cancer while awaiting retrial of his conviction of murdering the suspected killer of President Kennedy.

Who could not watch this fascinating drama playing out in the living room? We saw President Kennedy's wife Jackie in the dress with the blood stains (I would learn later that the dress was pink), Vice President Lyndon Johnson being sworn in as president aboard Air Force One, the coffin containing Kennedy's body arriving at Dover Air Force Base in Delaware. Then the funeral and the slow march of the procession to Arlington National Cemetery across the Potomac River in Virginia.

People Love a Conspiracy

The assassination of President Kennedy and the murder of the suspect, Lee Harvey Oswald, remained news for years. Conspiracy theories sprouted from all corners. "Grassy knoll" and "school book depository" and "pristine bullet" became parts of our language. A grainy, amateur video recorded by Abraham Zapruder, who was among the bystanders as the president's motorcade traveled through Dealey Plaza in Dallas, riveted us. It showed President Kennedy's body jolting from the impact of the bullets Oswald fired from his corner perch on the eighth floor of the school book storage building. Conspiracy theorists imagined plots carried out by Communists or the mob. They could offer slight evidence and no proof.

In my humble, but not uninformed opinion, Oswald acted alone. That was the conclusion of the Warren Commission, named after Chief Justice Earl Warren, which was appointed to study all of the information related to the assassination. I became convinced that Oswald acted alone after reading the 1993 book *Case Closed* by investigative reporter Gerald Posner. This coherent, compelling account of the assassination and the investigation reads easily. It was a finalist for the Pulitzer Prize. What convinced me that Oswald acted alone? Posner pointed out that Oswald began working at the book depository weeks before Kennedy's trip to Dallas and his motorcade route had been planned or announced. Oswald was a Communist. He hated the U.S. government and took advantage of circumstances. He much earlier had purchased a cheap rifle through a mail-order catalog, practiced shooting it rapidly and waited for a chance to strike. By simple chance, President Kennedy emerged as the ultimate target of opportunity.

In his epilogue to *Case Closed*, Posner postulated that people needed the assassination to be a conspiracy because they could not accept that, all by himself, a "pissant" like Oswald could so profoundly affect history. *Case Closed* would be a good read for anyone interested in American history. I loaned my copy of the book to a friend who lost track of it.

Grandpa Ford, who lived up the street from us, died three weeks after President Kennedy's death.

John-John's Salute

Many years later, a fellow member of my Optimist Club in Columbia, Missouri, shared an anecdote about the Kennedy funeral. My friend played trumpet in a military band. His unit played as pallbearers carried President Kennedy's coffin to a horse-drawn carriage for the procession to Arlington National Cemetery.

A famous photograph shows Kennedy's four-year-old son, called John-John at that time, saluting. The media gave the impression that the child was saluting the coffin as it passed out of the Capitol. My Optimist friend contradicted that. John-John was returning the salute of Charles de Gaulle, president of France, he said. The child probably saluted many times that morning, the coffin and de Gaulle among the recipients.

The Kennedy assassination and the persistence of the various conspiracy theories about the perpetrator(s) taught me a lesson that served me well over the years in my work as a newspaperman. Without realizing it at the time, I decided that how I thought and felt about things would depend upon facts. I would try to form my opinions, and certainly to write news, based upon the facts known at the time. I learned quickly after becoming a newspaper reporter that details of a story often change, sometimes quickly. A thick layer of fuzz can cover facts, especially when an elected official is involved. We all need to scrape away the fuzz.

A fact swirling around in the context of a situation can be seen from any direction. You can squint your eyes if you want to skew the facts or diminish their relevance to the context. I try to keep my eyes wide open and examine facts from various angles while trying to determine how important each fact is within the context of a situation.

An assignment while working in a journalism class at Central Missouri State University several years later demonstrated this idea for me. Our instructor assigned each of us to ask this question of ten random students on campus, without identifying them: "Have you ever smoked marijuana?"

The instructor got the idea after reading an article that stated that 15 percent of students at American colleges said they had smoked marijuana. This was the academic year 1967-68; marijuana use, although illegal, was growing rapidly during that time. Whether 15 percent of students – or more or fewer – had actually smoked marijuana wasn't relevant. That's the percentage of students who said they had smoked weed.

After the results of my class's survey were compiled, we were assigned to write a story about them. At the next session, the instructor told the class that I was the only one who had written the appropriate lead for the story. The other students opened their stories with something like: "Fifteen percent of CMSU students admit that they have smoked marijuana." My version of the story lead with: "The same percentage of CMSU students admit to having smoked marijuana as students on campuses across the country."

I'm a Lefty

On the occasions when I've discussed politics with people through the years, I tell them I'm a Democrat, just so they know, and try to explain why. "It's simple," I say. "I believe we get more things done and make things better for more people when we work together. The Democratic Party seems more inclined to do that. That's why I vote Democratic. Now, you tell me why you're a Republican (or whatever)."

The few who bother to explain their reasoning say government regulations smother the creativity and entrepreneurship of the individual, and high taxes suck the wind out of productivity. The smaller the government, the better. And they don't want unemployed deadbeats driving Cadillacs to get food stamps.

I respond by pointing out that the institutions and infrastructure of government, provided by the collective effort of the citizenry, help individuals and entrepreneurs realize their dreams. Rules and regulations are the result of abuses of the privilege of operating in a free country and harming the community of citizens that extended the privilege. The United States is a big country. It takes big government to protect the rights of each individual citizen from the abuses of privilege and quite often the tyranny of the majority. Majorities make the laws, but majorities can be and often are wrong. In theory, even a majority cannot deny the Constitutional rights of a lone U.S. citizen.

This country has enough wealth to provide a comfortable life for every man, woman and child in it. Massive wealth is like a black hole in space, it eventually sucks all other bits of money into it. Give a rich person a tax break and the money exits the economy and goes straight into a stock portfolio.

Give a poor person a monthly check and every penny goes immediately right into the local economy. What if one percent of our population began hoarding wholesome food, clean water or fresh air? How long would the 99 percent tolerate that? A "let them eat cake" attitude brought down the French monarchy. History contains lessons.

Deadbeats driving Cadillacs is a red herring.

Kennedy v. Nixon

One of my earliest memories involving presidential politics occurred on the election night of Kennedy vs. Nixon in November 1960. I was at a friend's house across the street, next door to the chicken butcherers. The friend and I often did homework together. His mom made popcorn and served iced tea with sugar in it. I never got sugar in iced tea at my house, which explains why I didn't drink iced tea at home.

Election results and commentary poured from the television. My friend and I sat on the living room floor while his father, sitting in his recliner, talked about the election and explained the process. I had never heard a grownup talk intelligently about politics in more than one sentence and with no cussing. It seemed intelligent to me, anyway.

Duck and Cover

The Cold War, and its thirty-year expansion of nuclear arsenals, began soon after World War II ended in 1945. In the 1950s, school children like me were taught to "duck and cover," as if cowering under our desks would shield us from a nuclear explosion. Some people, those with the money, the space and the most extreme fear, built underground bomb shelters and stocked them with water and canned goods.

Fear of nuclear holocaust provided fodder for an entire genre of Hollywood horror. What would happen if people survived the initial firestorms and fallout? What kind of fantastic creatures, spawned from nuclear radiation, would terrorize humanity? The Japanese film industry loved this theme. Me too. Invincible monsters breathing flame or shooting laser-beams out of their eyes emerge from the ocean and run amok in cities. For a time, they provided exciting Saturday-afternoon entertainment at the movie theater and late-night television viewing at home. Then I grew up some more and the monsters just looked goofy.

So far, negotiators and diplomats have pulled the world back from the brink of nuclear war. The spread of nuclear weapons had virtually ended, until now. Godzilla seems less of a threat these days, although he still draws at the box office. We'll soon learn what happens as countries allow arms-limitation treaties to expire.

Louie's

On a personal level, my descent into minor delinquency began in the midst of the Cold War era. That descent has a perfect metaphor: the stairway leading down to Louie's pool hall. Those stairs didn't descend far, one floor below ground level of downtown Grundy Center, and they didn't lead to a den of thieves or iniquity. They led to a narrow basement with a row of pool and snooker tables in the main room and a smaller room that held fewer than a handful of card tables. The card room lurked beneath the sidewalk in front of the shops along Main Street. A narrow street-level door between Manly's Rexall drug store and a small retail shop gave access to Louie's.

I misspent hours of my youth drinking five-cent fountain Cokes at the drug store and playing snooker in Louie's. During the week, after supper, I'd tell Mom and Dad I was going to a friend's house. I went to Louie's. Dad never told me directly, but my brother Scott said Dad didn't want us boys going to Louie's. Neither Dad nor Scott ever explained why. Our Dad didn't feel he had to explain himself beyond, "Because I said so."

Louie didn't sell beer. All you could do down there was play pool, smoke, and play cards, mostly a quick, simple game called Pepper. Maybe that's what Dad wanted to protect us from, the evils of Pepper. Well, it didn't work. Neither Scott nor I smoked first-hand, but growing up in a house with smokers and spending hours in the perpetual haze in Louie's provided plenty of second-hand exposure.

Scott taught me how to play snooker. I beat him my first game. Snooker resembles pool. You have to hit the balls into pockets. Making one of the red snooker balls allows you to shoot at a numbered ball. The balls and the pockets on a snooker table are slightly smaller than on a regular pool table. If you left the cue ball in position where your opponent did not have a clear shot at a red ball, you had "snookered" him.

My snooker skills suffered greatly after I got glasses. You would think a person with clear vision could shoot better pool, but the frames of my glasses required me to crane my neck at an uncomfortable angle. There's some irony, and who doesn't enjoy a bit of irony? I quit playing baseball because I couldn't see well enough without glasses. When I got glasses, my snooker game went south. Life's full of puzzling contradictions like that, enough to discourage a person lacking a sense of humor.

Louie's Learning Center

The fog of high school algebra lifted for me in Louie's. Because of my frequent presence, Louie – the owner's name really was Louie, an older man, and he was there much of the time – informally hired me to watch his counter while he played cards in the back room. While doing homework on the glass countertop, I sold candy bars and handed out trays of balls to pool and snooker players.

Few of my classes in school gave me much trouble, but algebra baffled me. The burden of introducing freshmen to algebra fell to the chemistry teacher, and that's about all he did, introduce us. "Here's your algebra book. Good luck." Maybe he didn't understand algebra either.

A senior noticed my frustration. "What's eating you?" he asked. "Algebra! I don't get it." The guy, a popular jock in school who knew me only as Scott Ford's little brother, came around the counter. He showed me how multiplying or dividing letters by other letters equal a number. Or some such magic. It clicked. That was the coolest thing any upperclassman ever did for a punk freshman. And it happened in Louie's! I passed algebra only because I disobeyed Dad.

The Fab Four

A rock band from England, The Beatles, hit the radio waves big around this time, 1963. Folks older than eighteen scoffed at the Brits because their hair hung down over their ears and hid their eyebrows. Hits also began escaping from another British group, the Rolling Stones, around then. It took me, a Beach Boys fan, several weeks to warm up to The Beatles. The release of "She Loves You" in 1963 didn't grab hold of me at first. It and later songs grew on me though, and I became a great fan of The Beatles over the next few years. I've still got twenty Beatles albums I bought in the 1960s.

The Rolling Stones' "Satisfaction," released in 1965, became my favorite song for several weeks. What was called "the British Invasion" virtually took over radio stations that played rock music. Bands from Great Britain played most of the songs on the radio for several years in the mid-Sixties. Millions of people, me among them, watched The Beatles on the Ed Sullivan Show on Sunday night television in February 1964.

Sparks in the Night

After my sophomore year of high school, Scott and I took a trip to Gladstone to visit our mother, Donna, and the Stewart family. Scott drove us down from Grundy Center in his 1957 Chevy. Darkness fell before we arrived. A slow-moving line of six or eight cars bogged us down on a hilly two-lane highway thirty miles from our destination. (Many four-lane highways were not built until after the mid-1960s.) The frustrating procession crawled into a long stretch between two shallow hills. With no headlights approaching, Scott jumped on the gas and pulled out to pass. As we reached the middle of the string of cars, one of them turned left. My breath caught and my back rammed the seat as I tried desperately to slow us down by stomping on the floorboard. My knuckles turned white as I braced for impact. The turning car smacked a glancing blow off the right side of Scott's car, sending us over the shoulder into a shallow ditch.

Never letting off the gas, Scott roared along the bottom of the grassy ditch and coolly sidled back onto the highway, scraping gravel and trailing sparks all the way. My right knee throbbed. It had been resting against the car door that got hit. Considering all of the things that could have killed us instantly – a tree, a driveway across the ditch or an oncoming car among them – a sore knee didn't seem worth complaining about.

After we calmed down a bit and discussed the situation, we decided we better go back to see what mayhem we had caused. Leaving the scene of an accident is a crime. There wasn't a car in sight at the scene. When we reached the Stewart house, Scott called the Highway Patrol to report the incident. That was the end of it, except for my knee, which ached for days, and the serious scrape on the side of Scott's sweet '57 Chevy.

I was reminded of this brush with death when Captain "Sully" Sullenberger landed his airliner in the Hudson River beside Manhattan after a flock of geese disabled the plane's engines just after takeoff. All 155 passengers and crew on board survived that extraordinary feat of cool-headedness in January 2009. If you trust your training and have confidence in your skill and your equipment, and if you don't panic in the face of extremes, it's amazing what you can power through. Throwing up your hands, closing your eyes and screaming in despair will lead to a less-than-optimal outcome.

Even if your brother takes your breath away with a quick peak at death, you've got to love him when he pulls you back from the pit. I mentioned earlier that Scott was born a Marine. This traffic scrape occurred shortly before he aged into the Corps, a perfect place for his aggressive nature. (Scott served three tours in Vietnam with a Marine air unit.)

Chapter 8

Forced Evacuation

D ad got a different job, again. He opened his own auto body shop in Grinnell, fifty miles south of Grundy Center. He drove to work every Monday through Saturday for months. Then, after my sophomore year in high school, during the spring of 1964, he moved the family to Grinnell. That embittered me. All my friends lived in Grundy Center. I knew nobody in Grinnell. Being a new kid in a town I didn't want to be in caused me to grow a chip of surliness that I wore defiantly on my shoulder. My smart-ass attitude must have appeared as lower-class resentment, teen-age rebellion or a blend of both.

Grinnell, a community of about 5,000, is home to the small, expensive, private liberal arts college named after it, Grinnell College. My family moved into another in a succession of well-worn, two-story frame houses. This one was three blocks from the college, near the east edge of town. The high school sprawled out on the west edge of town, a long walk, especially in winter. Fortunately, a couple of high school guys with cars also lived in my neighborhood. They were generous with rides.

As a businessman, Dad made a good body-and-fender man. He soon closed his shop and went to work at another body shop in town.

Sports Out, Work In

My feeble, half-hearted attempt to make the Grinnell wrestling team ended after only a few practices. Without friends it wasn't fun. The coach thought that a poor excuse for quitting after such a short trial. I had played football in Grundy Center, too, but I didn't even attempt that at Grinnell. I suspected the hulks from the big Des Moines schools that Grinnell played would make a cripple out of a 130-pounder like me. In retrospect, I shouldn't have played football at all, even in Grundy Center. My knees, shoulders and lower back make me groan and gimp.

Playing with friends made football fun in Grundy. I distinctly remember being disappointed if I didn't hurt somewhere after a football play, either at practice or in a game. If you didn't feel any pain, you hadn't been in on the action. Playing football in Grundy set me up for some success in Grinnell. I was a stud playing flag football in PE against kids who'd seldom held a football or run a wind sprint before. I picked off passes right and left, long and short, and spun out of most attempts to snatch a flag out of my waistband. The PE teacher told me I should go out for the football team. Too busy, I said.

Not being tied up with sports after school allowed me to get a steady job at a downtown restaurant, The Longhorn. That put spending money in my pocket and kept me from running amok full time.

Losing Control

During my junior year in high school, I totaled a friend's 1960 Ford Fairlane 500. While he was at work, he let me take his car for a spin. Another friend joined me, and we drove out of town on a gravel road that ran past his girlfriend's house not far into the country. We were cruising no more than forty miles per hour as we passed the girl's house on the left side of the road. I jerked my head to the left and said, "There it is!" When I jerked my head left, I also turned the steering wheel left, not a lot, but enough to point the car toward the ditch. I overcorrected to the right, fishtailed a couple of times on the loose gravel and went over the left edge of the road. The car plunged into a shallow ditch. The left front hit the embankment on the far side of the ditch, the car spun around and rolled backward.

When the car hit the embankment, the impact pitched me forward. My right cheek smashed against the rearview mirror, knocking me out for an instant. I didn't feel the impact of hitting the mirror, and I came to as the car jerked to a halt in the ditch. Blood poured from my cheek down the front of my shirt. My buddy's knees had hit the dashboard and his head the windshield. He had a headache for a couple of days, but nothing on him broke and he didn't bleed.

My friend got us out of the car and over to his girlfriend's house. One of the girl's parents drove us the couple of miles to a doctor's office in town. As he sewed up my cheek, the doctor tsk-tsked and complained about reckless teenage drivers who kept interrupting his quiet evenings at home.

Mom came to the doctor's office, consoled me after he bandaged my wound, and took me home. My cheek stung, but not nearly as much as the shame of wrecking a buddy's car and causing another friend's head to ache for days. My humiliation eased slowly in the following weeks. The scar on my cheek took much longer to fade.

On the Monday morning at school after the crash, the principal's secretary's voice came over the intercom after morning announcements. "Kent Ford please report to the principal's office." The principal chewed me out for crashing a car. "I hate going to funerals for students," he said. I had never felt one way or another about the principal until then. Now I hated him. Piling on someone who's down causes resentment.

One of the teachers at Grinnell High School made my list, too. He taught business classes and advised the student newspaper. I approached him one day, told him of my interest in newspapers and that I'd like to try my hand on the student journal. He was sorry, he said, but he didn't have any classes in newspaper production.

Every teacher can't be a "To Sir, With Love" high school hero, but is it too much to ask that all of them be at least a little encouraging?

Boss Takes Charge

My boss at The Longhorn helped me get over my guilt and anxiety over being a teenage car crasher. I had been washing dishes, bussing tables and cleaning up at the restaurant for a few months. I worked hard, showed up when scheduled and even filled in when someone else had something better to do. After the bandage and stitches were removed from my cheek, the boss put me right back to work bussing tables and washing dishes.

I objected to working in the dining room, saying people didn't want to see a kid with an angry gash on his cheek fussing around the tables while they ate dinner. He didn't buy that, saying nobody would pay any attention. Basically, "Get back to work."

He was wrong about nobody noticing. It didn't take long. One of the waitresses came into the kitchen and said a woman asked her who kissed the busboy, he has lipstick on his cheek. It wasn't lipstick, of course, it was the wound. Everyone in the kitchen chuckled, even me. The boss had used my situation to teach me the common lesson that you've got to get right back on the horse that throws you. These days, we call people like him a mentor. He remains more vivid in my memory than any of my school teachers.

Most of the servers at The Longhorn were high school girls. They all had senior boyfriends, but I swear all of them loved me a little. It probably had a lot to do with my enthusiasm as a busboy, keeping their customers' water glasses topped off, delivering salads and resetting tables quickly so hungry customers could be seated. Tips are a big deal to waitresses, and I helped ours rake them in. They shared a buck or two with me on occasion. I helped them do well, they appreciated it. That applies as long as those being helped realize their success isn't all of their own doing. Teamwork is powerful.

One of the waitresses begged me to take her weekend shift so she could go on a special date with her boyfriend, who was a stud of some kind in the high school, probably a jock. This waitress, a knockout, the popular Homecoming queen, had a million-dollar smile. She dangled bait. "I'll give you a kiss if you take my shift." With a bit more flirting she would have bare-hooked me, but I snapped up her offer.

When it came time for her to pay up, she and I, along with her boyfriend, walked around the corner of the restaurant into the parking lot. Having her boyfriend in tow suppressed my expectations. She stopped, turned around, planted a quick peck on my cheek and flashed her radiant smile.

Filipino Fling

The Longhorn had a Filipino cook with an ornery streak, just the kind of character who appealed to me. He was my size, height-wise, twice my size, weight-wise. He used his accent to his advantage. When he needed me to do something – fetch a package of meat from the cooler or wash a pot – he'd call my name. Instead of "Ford," it always came out "Fart." I'd give him a look; he'd shrug and say, "What?"

One day after a meal rush, we were talking in a wide hallway between the kitchen and the restrooms. Somehow, the issue of wrestling came up, including mention of specific holds and moves. That led to mention of the "full nelson" hold, which is illegal in high school wrestling because it can crack a kid's neck. A wrestler applies a full nelson from behind his opponent. He puts his arms under the other guy's shoulders and locks his hands on the back of the guy's neck.

With my former-second-team-wrestler swagger, I declared with a smirk, "You can't escape from a full nelson." "I can," the cook said nonchalantly. I don't recall if a bet ensued, but a challenge had been issued.

The cook turned his back to me and raised his arms. I moved in behind him and locked my hands behind his neck. A half second later I was lying on my back looking up at the cook. What could I do? I giggled. He had reached back over his head, grabbed me, dropped and flung. I didn't even have time to enjoy the ride.

Corvair Cruising

Another high school acquaintance, not a close friend of mine but a friend of friends, drove around in a white Chevrolet Corvair. The Corvair fit into the Volkswagen Beetle class – small, euphemistically called "compact" in auto-speak. Like the Beetle, its engine was in the rear, its trunk in front. The knucklehead who drove this Corvair and his associates got thrills by taking turns curling up and riding in the tiny trunk – the trunk in the front of the car. Whether I recognized the idiocy of what they were doing or just didn't have the nerve, I passed when my turn came.

The Corvair couldn't win a drag race. It had an engine slightly larger than a lawnmower's. With a teenager at the wheel, it still could drift sideways around street corners. About this time consumer advocate Ralph Nader wrote his book about General Motors, its Corvair and the U.S. auto industry in general, *Unsafe at Any Speed* (1965). Boy did he shake things up for car makers. To this day Ralph Nader rails against companies and industries that abuse their workers and dump dangerous and toxic products into the world.

Ralph Nader ran for president four times. By running as a Green Party candidate in the 2000 race, he won the presidency for Republican George W. Bush. The outcome of that election was not known for a couple of months, pending recounts of votes in Florida and the examination of that state's ballots with "hanging chads." (You'll have to look that up if you're interested.) The final official count in Florida showed Bush with about 500 more votes that his Democratic opponent, Al Gore.

Nader, a liberal like Gore, only more so, received 97,000 votes in Florida. Had Nader not been in the race, Gore would have received most of those votes, giving him a substantial margin over Bush. Al Gore would have been the 43rd president, not George W. Bush.

Chapter 9

The Future Looks Brighter

Well into my senior year at Grinnell High School, I didn't have any idea what I would do after graduation. Because grammar and writing came easily, and because the *Des Moines Register* paper route I handled for three years planted a seed, working for a newspaper had occurred to me. A plan to make that happen had yet to germinate. Going to college had never been a possibility, so it never entered my thoughts. After high school, I would see what came along.

Then my mother, Donna Stewart, came to see me. She had done this infrequently over the years, mostly because Dad and my stepmom, LaVelle, had made it clear to her that she was not welcome to visit my big brother Scott and me. Also, she had a family of her own back in Missouri. Those things didn't stop her though.

When I was younger, I didn't understand who the stranger named Donna was who came around once in a while and brought presents to Scott and me. Usually the appropriate age range of the mysterious gifts lagged behind our actual ages. When I was 10 Donna brought a Tonka dump truck, a great gift for a 7-year-old. Always those presents were more extravagant than anything we received at Christmas or on a birthday. Scott and I usually never got a glimpse of Donna on a visit, we just got the presents without knowing where they came from. Scott told me later he always knew.

When she came to see me in Grinnell, Donna – she was still Donna, not yet Mom to me – asked me what I planned to do after high school. I mentioned my vague thoughts about newspaper work. If that didn't work out, whatever presented itself.

"If you want to go to college, you can come and live with me and I'll help you," she said. That offer changed my life more than anything else. An entirely different future had become a possibility.

Quick Split

My mother, Donna (Martin), and my father, Harley, had married soon after Dad returned from the Army. Dad had served in a vehicle maintenance division in Europe during the closing months of World War II. Donna, a lively, attractive young woman, never lacked for boyfriends, according to her. She told about walking into the classroom at the beginning of a semester and a boy whistled. Instant boyfriend.

Donna told me she had decided, against her parents' wishes, to marry the first man who returned from the war and asked her to marry him. Harley was thirteen years older than Donna, but she liked his looks, and he asked the question. (My Aunt Jackie, Donna's youngest and only living sibling, told me on a visit to her home in Florida early in 2020 that Harley squatted in the Martin family's house for several weeks until Donna agreed to marry him.)

Impulsiveness seldom leads to solid results, especially in relationships. My father and mother divorced when we lived in Wellsburg, Iowa, a couple of years after I was born.

Dad then started dating LaVelle Bausman, Scott's and my babysitter. Dad needed someone to take care of his young boys while he was at work. LaVelle became our stepmother on May 10, 1951. LaVelle miscarried a boy, then had three children, my two half-sisters, Candace and Karin, and half-brother, Kevin, who came along between the two girls.

On June 10, 1980, LaVelle died of pancreatic cancer. She was 48. When diagnosed in 1979, LaVelle told doctors she wanted no radiation or chemotherapy. She is buried in the Ford family plot in the cemetery at Grundy Center, Iowa, alongside Kim, her miscarried son.

Donna had come to Grinnell with her proposition to help me attend college in 1965.

My First Real Wheels

I got my first car in Grinnell. Wheels had always provided escape. In Iowa you could get a driver's license on your sixteenth birthday. Before that age, bicycles took me, my brother and other juvenile escapees to fishing holes, muddy creeks and swimming pools within fifteen miles of our hometown. We had breakdowns, but our thumbs got us close to home. A bicycle, though, won't get you much farther than the next town, if it's nearby, but that's what you get when you're a kid, a bicycle. By the time I reached high school, nobody rode a bicycle to school. Uncool. If an upperclassman with a car wasn't around, and usually they weren't around me, I walked.

The 1953 scratch-and-dent, flathead Ford Fairlane I bought had bald tires all around, rust cavities in the floorboard and vapor-lock in its constitution. Seat belts? Don't be silly. I got the car early in 1966, a few months before high school graduation. Cockeyed alignment governed its speed. At forty miles per hour, a discreet rhythmic vibration crept up the steering column. At fifty, chaos broke out. Hanging on became an issue. I persevered. Being young helped.

The man I bought my four-wheeled freedom from lived across town, near the high school. He had painted the car a dull, multi-hued silver, with a brush. He hadn't bothered masking or detailing and obviously didn't care if subsequent brush strokes applied more or less tint than previous strokes, resulting in a unique aspect. He wanted sixty dollars, so that's what I paid.

I had a job washing dishes and bussing tables three miles south of town near the Interstate and a girlfriend twelve miles in the country northeast of town. I needed wheels. I would have paid seventy-five dollars for the forlorn Ford, probably. An insurance agent downtown sold me six months' worth of liability for ninety dollars. I considered it less of a bargain at half again the cost of the car, but it covered me through summer.

Now I asked myself: What can I do to spiff up this feeble sixty-dollar heap that I would drive to school, to work and to pick up my girl? What I did was paint red stripes across the top. (If your sow's not pretty, put a ribbon on it!) My dad was a body-and-fender man, car bodies were in our blood.

I used newspaper and tape to mask a four-inch stripe from the front bumper, up over the top and across the trunk to the back bumper, skipping over the windows. Then I masked a narrower stripe a couple of inches parallel to the first stripe, and sprayed the paint. Those red omens of menace curved smoothly from the right edge of the hood toward the center of the roof and back to the right. Not exactly what I was going for, but the sweeping arc provided a custom touch, rakish.

My chariot lacked a vital hot-weather accessory. Not air conditioning, a jug of water. Summer came and my sweet escape became an old gray mule. That is to say, stubborn. It quit and would not go without a cooling splash. A new fuel pump would have prevented the vapor-lock, but fuel pumps weren't free like water. Whenever the car decided it was too hot to go on, it quit. Wherever we were, there we were. This became so routine that I didn't even cuss any more when it happened. I grabbed the jug off the back floorboard, opened the hood and poured a pint of water over the fuel filter housing. After a minute or two the vapor in the housing condensed, allowing fuel to flow, and off we went, the mule and me.

The silver rust-bucket got me to my job washing dishes and bussing tables at the restaurant in a hotel along I-80 three miles south of Grinnell. The same man I had worked for at The Longhorn in downtown Grinnell ran this restaurant. I always showed up on time, tackled with enthusiasm sinks piled full of greasy pots and pans and pitched in when anyone needed a hand. The boss liked that, so when he moved his operation from The Longhorn downtown to the hotel south of town, he took me along. I got eighty cents an hour at The Longhorn, he paid me eighty-five cents at the new place. Restaurant people work hard. I've always enjoyed working with people who know their stuff and get to it. It's fun to be a part of that.

My silver heap also got me out toward Montezuma, a small town east of Grinnell. (I registered for the draft at the courthouse in Montezuma after my eighteenth birthday.) My girlfriend lived on a farm near Montezuma. That meant gravel roads. Driving on gravel roads in a car with holes in the floorboard makes your teeth gritty. Carpet scraps deflected the clouds a bit.

The radio worked in spite of the road dust and the misalignment shimmy. Bob Dylan's "Everybody Must Get Stoned" climbed the charts that summer. It became my anthem. I never was a stoner, but I liked the twangy thump of the tune and the wigged-out lyrics. I considered myself something of a rebel drifting around those gravel curves in my silver hotrod, heading to pick up my girl, chewing dust.

That was my last summer as an Iowan. I was heading to Gladstone, Missouri, to live with my mother, Donna. I had enrolled for the fall semester at Metropolitan Junior College in Kansas City.

Donna came to Grinnell to pick me up. She followed me and the heap to the scrapyard south of town, out toward the restaurant where I worked. I drove in and parked. "How much will you give me for it?" I asked. I thought fifteen dollars a bit low, but I had no bargaining position. I put the five and the ten in my pocket and got into Mother's car, a smooth, clean, yellow-and-white Oldsmobile. She drove south.

Chapter 10

Going to Kansas City, Almost

Donna's family consisted of her husband, Charles Robert Stewart, known as "Bob" by members of his family and "Charlie" by many of his work associates; her delightful young daughters, my half-sisters Jackie and Valerie, and a verging-on-vicious, black-and-brown wiener dog named Dan.

I don't know how Bob felt about suddenly having an 18-year-old male move into his house, but he and I always got along well. Jackie and Valerie, who were in elementary school, have told me they loved having a big brother. I cut the grass, painted bedroom walls and drove the girls to their activities.

The small ranch-style house in Gladstone, a northern suburb of Kansas City, had a tiny finished room in the attic with a twin bed, a dresser and a small desk and chair. That's where I lived after I joined the Stewarts. The unfinished basement had a convenient showerhead hanging from a ceiling rafter, and the fenced backyard provided Dan with a place to sniff around and conduct dog business.

My classes at Metropolitan Junior College began soon after I moved in with my new family. Bob and I went down to the Volkswagen dealer in North Kansas City. He bought a new creamy-white Beetle off the lot for $1,650. On weekdays I drove that car across the ASB Bridge over the Missouri River and through downtown Kansas City to school.

A United Parcel Service warehouse loomed adjacent to the south end of ASB bridge. I got a part-time, union-dues-paying job there unloading packages from collection trucks and loading them into trucks that would deliver them all around northwest Missouri.

Howling With the Wolfpack

I had been a pro football fan for several years. Bart Starr and the Green Bay Packers were my favorite team, mostly because they won a lot and seemed to be on television more than other teams. Them and the Chicago Bears. I also liked the Washington Redskins for some reason, perpetual losers back then, and quarterback Johnny Unitas and his Baltimore Colts.

After moving in with the Stewart family, I joined the Wolfpack, as fans of Len Dawson and the Kansas City Chiefs were known. A person wearing a costume resembling a cartoonish wolf performed mascot antics during games. Still does. After each Chiefs' score, a nearly naked man dressed as an Indian, complete with war paint, streaming headdress and feathered spear, rode a paint horse around the field. That tradition ended some years back.

The Chiefs won the American Football League championship in 1966, coinciding perfectly with my relocation to Missouri. On January 15, 1967, at Memorial Coliseum in Los Angeles, the Chiefs played the Packers in the annual game that soon would be officially named the Super Bowl. The Chiefs lost 35-10.

Before the game, the city of Kansas City held a rally for the Chiefs on the grounds of the Liberty Memorial downtown. Thousands of people packed the hillside below the memorial tower. During the rally, organizers unspooled a roll of yellow Western Union telegram paper down the hill through the crowd. Those who could reach the paper signed the telegram, which extended hopes for victory to the team in Los Angeles. I signed the telegram.

Three years later I watched snippets of the rematch in an airplane hangar at Lemoore Naval Air Station in California. More on that to come.

From Gladstone to Brookfield

Bob, my stepdad, worked for Western Union in Kansas City for several years. Donna worked at the North Kansas City headquarters of Farmland Industries, an agriculture co-op. Bob left Western Union and became an advertising sales representative for magazines catering to cattle farmers in the Midwest. The magazine work required hours of highway travel, but no need to live in Gladstone. Late in the summer of 1967 the Stewarts with me in tow moved to Brookfield, a town of five thousand in north central Missouri.

Bob grew up on the Stewart family farm a mile east of Sumner, a tiny community a few miles southwest of Brookfield. Donna's family during much of her childhood lived in Atlanta, Missouri, a burg on Highway 63 between Kirksville and Macon in northern Missouri.

Central Missouri Sophomore

I enrolled for my sophomore year at Central Missouri State University in Warrensburg. CMS (now the University of Central Missouri) was a suitcase university. Students lived in dormitories, but every Friday afternoon streams of cars headed out of Warrensburg toward hometowns in all directions.

Johnson County exploited the weekly ritual of thousands of students racing toward friends, family and home cooking. Speed traps snagged those accelerating toward escape velocity. A deputy parked on the back side of a hill radared vehicles and radioed ahead. A half-mile farther up the road co-conspiring deputies waved speeders off the road and issued citations. Johnson County officials no doubt said great things about higher education. It provided a tidy revenue stream.

The Stewarts moved into a two-story white frame house on Main Street just north of the downtown city park. That house fell victim to the expansion of the nearby Baptist Church parking lot many years ago.

Me and the Volkswagen in a Brookfield city park. My future wife, Sharon Blankenship, took the picture.

Terror at the Drive-in

One weekend three of my borderline delinquent friends from college and I carried out a nighttime raid in Brookfield. The mayhem we caused didn't hurt anyone or damage any property, but it certainly brought things to a halt. The statute of limitations must be in effect by now, but just in case, the names of my accomplices die with me.

A volatile combination of cabin and spring fevers might explain our behavior. That combination provides a plausible excuse. There is no good excuse, but we were males of a certain age unsupervised by an adult or a female friend who had matured beyond us. If any one of us had had a girlfriend at that time, our commando team would have been drained of manpower. If you had a girlfriend, you didn't hang out with other delinquents, especially on weekends. We could have recruited more troops if they hadn't had dates. Some of those potential guerillas probably went to the drive-in theater that night.

We had fled academic confinement for the weekend. Scuffing along a gravel road near Brookfield, we pretended to hunt squirrels and asked one another what we were going to do with ourselves for two days.

Idea Sprouts, Blossoms

One of the guys said we could shoot some fireworks. He had a sack of cherry bombs, and he yearned to hear them explode. In case you've never seen one, they are called cherry bombs because they look like cherries.

Whose idea this was really doesn't matter, there's culpability aplenty. The idea grew wings. It didn't take long before we had laid out a mission that demanded greater-than-average swagger and less-than-average good sense. We had both, what could go wrong?

The Target: The drive-in theater occupied a couple of acres at the west edge of town. Drive-ins attracted hordes of people on warm evenings during the 1960s. They provided a secure make-out alternative to isolated gravel roads. That impression of security suffered a blow this night.

The Plot: Sneak in, stroll around dropping lit cherry bombs, sneak back out.

Cigarettes were key. A cigarette will stay lit and burn slowly if nobody is smoking it. They make great delay fuses for cherry bombs and the like.

Brookfield's drive-in sat catty-corner from a service station and diner where partiers and other prowlers went for late-night gasoline, burgers and fries. Pastures buffered the drive-in. A dropsied barbed-wire fence provided feeble protection from determined sneakers-in.

Our squad bided its time, letting the night's movie advance well into its plot. We knew that by then the windows on many of the vehicles in the drive-in would be fogged over from the heavy breathing of the teen-agers making out inside.

After a brief reconnoiter, we parked down the road along the west edge of the theater grounds. Three of us left the get-away car, crept along the fence to the back corner, slipped over the sagging wires and dispersed into the darkness that shrouded the vehicles in the theater.

Our pockets bulged with cherry bombs. One saboteur covered the gravel paths in the front near the screen. My assignment, the center rows. Our third raider sowed the back drives with explosives. We had divvied up the ordnance, and each of us carried a pack of cigarettes. At this point in the operation, it became every man for himself if something went wrong.

We did not know how long it would take to light ten cigarettes and stick fuses of the cherry bombs into them while walking quickly in the dark. We did know we had to get out of the drive-in before the first bomb exploded.

The muted dialogue and soundtrack of the movie coming from the speakers hanging on car windows were the only sounds in the nearly full theater grounds. Moving quickly, but trying not to draw attention, I lit cigarettes, tore off the filters, stuck cherry bomb fuses into them, placed them gently on the ground and moved on. Nobody called out or honked. A person walking fast in a drive-in usually indicates a trip to the snack bar or restroom. No commotion erupted from my partners' sectors.

My circuit up one gravel drive and back on the one behind it took only a couple of minutes. The three of us arrived back at the fence corner nearly simultaneously. We hunkered down, ran to the get-away car and drove straight to the truck stop, where we parked facing the drive-in.

Then, CHAOS! Girls screamed. Boys shouted curses as explosion after explosion rocked the theater. Oh, the humanity! The pandemonium we had wrought awed us. We whooped and hollered. Nobody high-fived back then, it hadn't been invented yet, but we congratulated each other enthusiastically over our successful mission.

It took less than a minute for all of the cherry bombs to go off. The investigation started immediately. Lights came on in the drive-in. Excited people stood around jabbering as cars streamed out the gate onto the highway.

Like criminals returning to the scene of their crime, we wanted a closer look at the turmoil. We acted like regular guys arriving for the late show and drove in against the flow. A scowling man with a flashlight walked alongside the line of slow-moving cars exiting the drive-in grounds. He looked closely into all of the cars.

"Show me your hands," he growled as he shined the light into our car. "Oh, crap," I thought, "he's checking for gun powder." Somehow, we passed his inspection. He told us the drive-in was closed. We turned around and drove into the night.

I don't know if Brookfield's *Daily News-Bulletin* printed a story with a headline like "Stealth Bombers Shut Down Drive-in," but it missed a good one if it didn't.

Dr. King and Bobbie Killed

About the same period of time as the drive-in raid, four of us sat around a table playing cards in a dormitory lounge at Central Missouri. We were the only ones in the room. Someone opened a door to the lounge, poked his head in and told us the Rev. Dr. Martin Luther King Jr. had been shot and killed in Memphis. It was April 4, 1968. One of the card players made a crude comment. I pointed out that Dr. King preached non-violence, and bad things could happen. Rioters burned buildings in many cities around the country.

Two months later, on June 6, Bobbie Kennedy was assassinated in the kitchen of a hotel in Los Angeles. He had just won the California Democratic primary election for president.

As that summer of 1968 progressed, my relationship with Sharon Blankenship, my future wife, warmed up. We had been introduced by my college mates when we were home from Warrensburg one weekend. Sharon's family and my family lived only five blocks apart in Brookfield.

CHAPTER 11

FLOUNDERING IN LOCUST CREEK

My canoe needs a biography. The saga would feature an ill-advised, potentially tragic adventure that occurred when we lived in Brookfield.

My canoe has been hauled around Missouri on top of one vehicle or another for floats in various rivers, on loan to brother Scott who used it in Iowa for a few years, and sunken in a flooded creek and recovered with the help of an air search.

I bought the canoe in 1967 during the time I lived with the Stewarts in Gladstone. The sixteen-foot square-back canoe hung suspended from the ceiling in a Montgomery Ward store. A significant scratch marred the starboard side of the vessel, which I pointed out to a store clerk. That scratch scratched a hundred dollars off the price, so I hauled the canoe home.

The Stewart family moved to Brookfield late in the summer of 1967, just before I started my sophomore year at Central Missouri State in Warrensburg. Several other guys in nearby dorm rooms were from Brookfield or smaller towns in that area. We went home on many weekends.

A couple of the guys and I thought it would be cool to take a short float on Locust Creek, which flows mostly southward about five miles west of Brookfield. Late in the afternoon three of us strapped the canoe to the top of the Stewart's Volkswagen and packed it to Pershing State Park. Locust Creek flows through the park. We parked the VW beside a bridge over the creek a mile south of Pershing Park and rode back to the canoe in a second vehicle.

Second Thoughts? Anyone?

It needs to be mentioned here that we had a case of beer. A couple of other things need to be mentioned. One of the guys confessed that he couldn't swim very well. And, as a result of heavy spring rains, the creek was near flood stage and flowing briskly. Life jackets had never crossed our minds, so we didn't have any.

None of us wanted to acknowledge this recipe for disaster. Alcohol wasn't a factor, because we hadn't drunk any of the beer yet. But the overloaded canoe in the rolling creek made an ominous combination that we ignored. We shoved off with me at the stern, one of the other guys with a paddle on the front seat and the third guy perched on the bar across the beam, the case of beer between his legs.

Locust Creek meanders through the bottoms like a sidewinder rattlesnake slithering across dessert sand. We didn't know that. This winding course added another ingredient to our stew of foolishness. We couldn't see around the bends of the creek. In a canoe on a stream, seeing what's ahead has advantages. You can make adjustments.

It didn't take long for our adventure to deteriorate along with the daylight. The stream shot us around a bend to the right and turned us sideways. Before we could straighten out, our port side smashed into a pile of brush in the middle of the creek. The canoe listed hard. Instinctively, all three of us leaned hard right. We should have done something else. The canoe pitched to starboard and flooded immediately. I grabbed our only flashlight from my pocket and flung it toward the bank twenty feet away. It flew about eighteen feet and splashed into the current.

Because the canoe and the brush pile blocked a route to the east bank, we plunged into the water and flailed toward the west bank. Spurred on by panic, all three of us quickly made the short swim and scrambled up the muddy bank, soaked and shivering but relieved to be alive. The guy who couldn't swim very well got there first.

Locust Creek now flowed between us and the blacktop that runs through Pershing Park. The canoe slipped around the snag and drifted down the creek, only its bow visible.

We quickly assessed our situation in what little remained of daylight. If we followed the creek, even in the dark, we soon would come to the bridge where we had left the car. It wasn't that far, if you happen to be a crow. We could have swum back across to the east side of the creek and walked out to the blacktop. But because one of the guys didn't swim well and none of us wanted to get back into the cold rushing creek in the dark, we quickly dismissed that option. Besides, if we just stuck to the creek we would soon be to the car. An easy call.

Situation Deteriorates

Our circumstances faded along with the last of the daylight. In the growing darkness we made slow progress picking our way through the tangle of thorny brush and snagging vines that choke the woods along Locust Creek. When total darkness engulfed the woods, we lost the little momentum we had. We could no longer see obstacles in front of us.

You might think things couldn't get worse. Well, things can always get worse. As I attempted to plunge through a snag, a twig reached under my glasses and flung them into the night. Before that, all I could see was darkness, now the darkness was blurry. Searching for my glasses in that impenetrable jumble of underbrush would be futile.

After an hour or two of picking our way along the creek, we surrendered. Wrapped in the pitch black of the thick woods and trapped in the tangle, we decided to hunker down and wait for morning.

Bedding Down in the Bushes

The spring evening air chilled us in our wet clothes. We determined to start a fire. The soggy woods offered little dry fuel, so we dug our wallets out of our clammy pants hoping something had remained dry. A couple of small photographs and a receipt of some kind gave us hope. One of us had a cigarette lighter. Rooting around we gathered handfuls of dead twigs and tree litter. Eventually, blowing gently, we coaxed a spark into a flame. We laid down in a triangle as close to the tiny fire as possible and shivered through the night. When dawn finally broke, we discovered we had bedded down five feet from the edge of the roiling creek.

We fought our way out of the tangle to find the fields flooded in all directions. For what must have been two hours we slogged around looking for high ground, a fence or a road that would provide some hint of progress. Finally, we stumbled onto a country road and followed it until we came to a farmhouse. I can't imagine what the man thought when he found three muddy, soaking strangers standing on his doorstep. We explained our plight and asked for a ride to our vehicle in Pershing Park. The man obliged, probably thinking he'd hear a good story on the way.

The three us, wet and worn out, were soon warming up in our vehicles and heading home to Brookfield. Nobody in the Stewart household realized that I had been out all night, so no search patrols had been dispatched. If the other two guys were missed, I didn't hear about it.

That morning the family went to visit my stepfather Bob's brother, my Uncle Bill, and Aunt Bessie Stewart at the farm near Sumner. The farm is five miles down the road from Pershing Park. Locust Creek flows into Grand River just northwest of Sumner. Bill was Bob's older brother by a couple of years.

Naturally, the story of my hair-brained adventure came out. "Whatever possessed you to float on the flooding creek, in the dark?" Bill asked. What he meant was, "You idiot!"

When Uncle Bill asked where the canoe was, I said it had floated off, and we never looked for it. I assumed I'd never see the canoe again, supposing it to be well on its way to the Missouri River. But Uncle Bill knew Locust Creek. "I bet it's snagged not far from where you got dumped out," he said. Bill called another farmer he'd known for years who lived up the road a couple of miles. The farmer housed a two-seater airplane in a shed near his house.

Aerial Search

In no time at all I found myself seated beside the man, whom I'd never met before, as he bounced his tiny craft down a rough dirt lane in the middle of a cornfield. He didn't comment about the rough ride, so I figured it was routine for his takeoffs. But I would have appreciated some reassurance about his one-handed wrangling of the airplane. A sling constrained his right arm. He didn't say a thing about it, just barreled across the cornfield. He wrestled the plane into the air with no more thought than he would give to a quick drive to town for a part to fix a combine.

It took only a few seconds to reach the sky over Locust Creek just to the west of the man's farm. I told him where we'd put the canoe in, he tipped the plane on its side and began making sharp, slow turns a few hundred feet above the creek. It then became apparent why we had not been able to walk out of those woods. Locust Creek bends, a lot. By following the creek, all we had done was loop back and forth. We had struggled a hundred feet east and west for every fifty feet we had gained to the south, our direction of interest.

We hadn't made more than three or four sweeps over the creek when the pilot said, "There it is!" It took me a few moments to see it, a tiny wedge of bright silver protruding from the brown ribbon of the meandering creek. The bow of the canoe had snagged on a branch of a dead tree that had fallen into the stream. I marveled at how in the world the man had seen that glint of silver. He knew better than I what to look for.

Another marvel occurred when the farmer, with his one good arm, landed us safely back at his farm a minute or two later. He acted as though it had been a purely routine Sunday-morning errand. The man called the Stewart farm and told Uncle Bill exactly where he spotted the canoe just beyond the end of a trail that provided machinery access to a field. Bill knew the spot.

Stepdad Bob, Uncle Bill and a couple of others I don't remember piled into pickup trucks and headed north up the blacktop. It seemed to me a larger crew than necessary, but the situation offered a ready distraction from a mundane Sunday morning, something to gossip and snicker about.

The farmer and I met the group where the field path turned off the blacktop. We all drove to the end of the path and parked near the bank of Locust Creek. Upstream only a hundred yards the bow of the canoe stuck out of the water, looking somewhat larger than it had from above.

Morning Swim

Unfortunately, the canoe had hung up only a few feet from the opposite bank of the creek. The creek level had subsided somewhat since the previous night, and a gravel and mud bar emerged from our side of the stream opposite the snagged canoe.

Uncle Bill handed me one end of a rope and said, "Go get it." Standing on the gravelly mud bar I undressed slowly, down to my underpants, somewhat embarrassed by the situation and the audience, apprehensive of the task, and chilled by the cool air and the thought of getting into the frigid water.

"What are you waiting for?" Uncle Bill barked. "Get your ass in there!" He sensed I needed encouragement.

I walked a few feet to the upstream end of the mud bar and crept into the water. Letting the current do most of the work, a few breaststrokes got me across the creek to the canoe. I tied the rope to the canoe and wrestled it off the snag. We dragged it onto the mud bank and tipped out the water. I floated the canoe down to where the trucks were parked.

I learned a couple of lessons from this misadventure and got reminders of others. Look at the big picture before you leap, look again if your first look raises a red flag. Changing your mind almost always is an option, and sometimes is the right thing to do. Someone has to take charge. Don't assume too quickly that all is lost. Your family and friends will be there even when you can't imagine why they would be.

Sawmilling and Surveying

During my sophomore year at Central Missouri in Warrensburg, my enthusiasm for college waned, and the prospect of a draft to provide troops for the Vietnam War became real. Talk of a draft had swirled around Congress and the country for months. If I wasn't in college, the Army might send me into the jungle. I dodged the draft by joining the Navy. But that didn't happen until November that year, 1968.

I had two jobs in Brookfield before I joined the Navy. My first job involved the mindless hoisting of chunks of white oak onto a saw table at a mill a mile east of Brookfield. The mill produced staves for whiskey barrels and flat boards for barrel tops and bottoms. Brainless work, but definitely not brawnless. Oak is heavy. The word musclebound has never been used to describe me, but I could handle the chunks the barrel ends were cut from.

A crew of half a dozen ragged men ran the mill. The work was hard, especially if you were hung over. Sometimes one or two of the crew didn't show up for work. On one of those days I had to fill in at the big saw where oak logs were cut into staves, the slats used to make the body of a barrel.

Like factories everywhere, volume mattered. That hungry saw blade spun constantly, and the boss wanted logs on the rollers to feed it. Gaps meant wasted time. I wrestled logs onto the rollers until I couldn't do it by myself any longer. A guy from the saw crew inside the mill came to help. He helped me hoist logs onto the rollers until my body shut down. I had never before and have never since been so completely, totally, utterly exhausted. I wobbled. Lifting anything was out of the question. For the last hour of the shift I slumped like a corpse on a stack of logs.

My family rescued me from that daily punishment. We all rode in the family sedan to Los Angeles to visit the Martin family, Mother's kin. I used the trip as an excuse to retire from sawmilling. On that trip out west I met several aunts, uncles and cousins and saw the Rocky Mountains and the Pacific Ocean for the first time. We didn't go to Disneyland, but we did go to Knott's Berry Farm, another popular theme park in the Los Angeles area.

Blazing a Trail

When we returned to Brookfield, I hired on with a crew surveying the route of a future power line. My job amounted to helping the crew of four clear a line of sight through weeds, bushes and trees so the crew leader could chart elevations from one point to the next along the power line right-of-way.

I joined the crew as it worked through a grove of trees in the Locust Creek bottom west of Brookfield. Just before my time to report to the Navy in November, we reached Thomas Hill Reservoir twenty-five miles east of Brookfield. A power plant there produces the electricity that flows over the line we plotted. If you drive west from Brookfield on Highway 36 you pass under the power line about five miles from town.

I became close friends with the only other guy on the survey crew who lived in Brookfield. Before sunup on the morning of the day I went to St.

Louis for induction into the Navy, my surveying friend and I paddled my canoe across the Brookfield reservoir and squatted in the brush. I shot the only duck, a scaup, that flew past. We went home, then I went into the Navy.

Chapter 12

Dodging the Draft

In the 1960s, during the Vietnam War, a young man could get a deferment from military duty if he was attending college. Military deferments may be what made attending college an appealing thing to do. It also helped explain why African American men made up a much larger percentage of active duty military than their percentage of the population.

Attending public universities at that time did not require going deeply into debt. You could almost pay for the next term by working through the summer and holding a part-time job while in school. Almost. Most of the young people being funneled into the Vietnam War came from lower-income families, those who couldn't afford college. If your family had money, you could go to college forever, if necessary, to avoid being sent into combat.

I didn't want to combat anyone, and I didn't want anyone combatting me, so I dodged the draft by joining the Navy. It was November 1968. I was 20 years old. The Vietnam War draft lottery, the first since the end of World War II, didn't actually begin until December 1969. The war had become so unpopular that young men were not enlisting in the numbers required by the Army and Marines.

All men, when they reach age eighteen, are required to register for what's euphemistically called Selective Service. If the government activates a draft, all of those registered are candidates. Although many women now volunteer to serve in the military, they are not required to register for the draft when they reach age 18. Must be an oversight.

In the Vietnam War lottery, draftees were selected by day of birth. Numbers were drawn for each day of the year. Speculation ran that anyone whose birth date had a number up to about fifty stood a good chance of being drafted. My birth date, April 6, drew a number somewhere in the neighborhood of 240. That meant I had about the same chance of being drafted as winning the Power Ball lottery, much closer to no chance than slim chance. It didn't matter; I had already been in the Navy for a year.

The draft ended January 27, 1973, after many young American men had fled to Canada to avoid being called up. On that day President Richard Nixon signed the Paris Peace Accords ending our country's involvement in the Vietnam War. A couple of years later, in April 1975, Communist forces seized Saigon, the capital of South Vietnam. Soon after that, North and South Vietnam merged with the name Socialist Republic of Vietnam. Saigon became Ho Chi Mihn, named for the man who led the North Vietnamese Army during many years of the war in Southeast Asia.

We're Engaged

I had given my girlfriend, Sharon Blankenship, an engagement ring only a few days before I left for the Navy. Sharon and I were on our way in the Volkswagen Beetle to the Wild Goose Festival in Sumner. I stopped the car in the middle of the road just after I picked up Sharon at her house and gave her the ring. It wasn't a complete surprise, she helped pick out the ring at the local jewelry store. You had to squint to see the diamond, but not because of its massive brilliance. It was all I could afford. Sharon said she loved it.

The Beatles song "Hey Jude" hit the charts that August of 1968. Hearing that song reminds me of that period in my life, my engagement to Sharon, my work in Brookfield and the beginning of my time in the Navy. Sharon and I still smile when we hear it.

An Easy Choice

In my snot-nosed, pimply years I had sniffed lots of glue assembling plastic models of warplanes and aircraft carriers. Glue sniffing for its own sake didn't become a thing until some years later, and I don't think glue sniffers were into building models. Maybe the glue tricked my brain into thinking sticking tiny pieces of plastic together was fun. I remember the smell. We lived a thousand miles from the nearest sea, and I'd never seen a real warplane. Even so, nobody suggested that my gluing together small plastic ships and airplanes was any goofier behavior than my usual.

That youthful pursuit planted the seed of what would grow into my decision to enlist in the Navy. Similarly, my *Des Moines Register* paper route in Grundy Center set me on the path to a career in newspapers. A newspaper still seems like a miracle to me, at least of the minor category.

After my sophomore year in college, at Central Missouri State University in Warrensburg, I told the Navy recruiter in Brookfield that I'd join up if I could work on airplanes on a carrier. He said something like, "That can be arranged."

Great Lakes in Winter

My Navy career began the day of the 1968 presidential election between Democrat Hubert Humphrey, whom I wanted to win, and Richard Nixon, who did win. At that time you had to be 21 to vote. (Congress passed the twenty-sixth amendment to the Constitution in 1970, lowering the voting age to 18.) My mother, Donna Stewart, drove me to Moberly to meet my recruiter. He drove me to the Induction Center in St. Louis.

After cursory head-to-tail examinations by bored medical people, I and a few dozen other apprehensive-looking young men took the oath to protect our country and became Navy recruits. Election returns were broadcast at the induction center. They disappointed me. We recruits boarded a train in downtown St. Louis and headed north to Chicago. From the train station in the Windy City, buses took us several miles farther north to Great Lakes Naval Training Center on the western shore of Lake Michigan.

Winter at Great Lakes Naval Training Center in northern Illinois brought back bad memories of frozen fingers and toes on my paper route in central Iowa. Basic training consisted of mindless marching, endless physical examinations and countless hours waiting in chow and inoculation lines.

Recruits formed companies of about 120 men. We slept on thin mattresses in bunk beds with one sheet and one wool blanket. I learned to sleep lying on my back with the blanket tented from my toes to my arms folded across my chest to eliminate as much itch as possible.

Each man had a small locker beside his bunk. The lockers contained everything we needed during boot camp. We got step-by-step instructions on how to fold our shirts and pants so they would fit neatly into our lockers and pass inspections. With two years of college in my resume, clothes folding came easily to me.

A Mercenary

I entered the Navy with the mindset of making it an adventure, something to add depth and breadth to my life experience. I did not support the Vietnam War, but with the draft approaching, I did not want to be swept up by the Army and sent into the jungles of Southeast Asia.

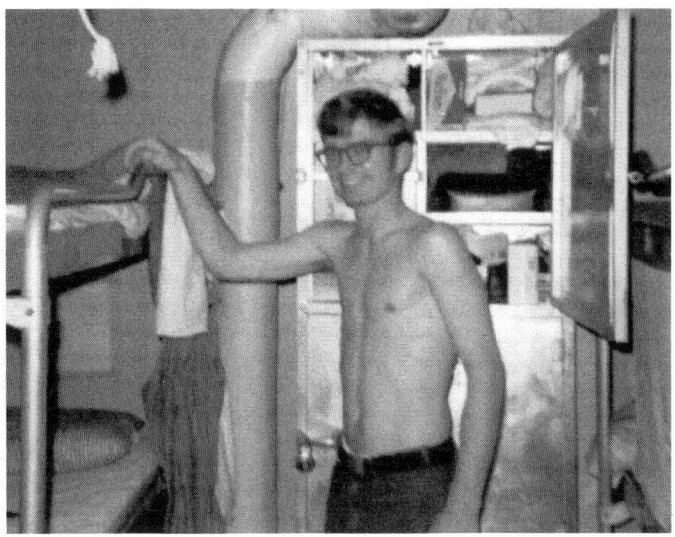

Me, my locker and my rack in the barracks during basic training at Great Lakes Naval Training Center north of Chicago. My company hadn't been to the barbershop yet. We were still getting step-by-step instructions on how to properly fold our pants and shirts, training that went overboard immediately upon graduation from boot camp.

Also, military service would qualify me for GI Bill benefits. Those benefits included payment for college. After my first two years of college, I had lost interest and needed a break from the classroom. Military service offered a way to finish a degree later. I joined the Navy for the adventure and the money. In effect, I was a mercenary.

That reality caused me emotional turmoil for many years. My participation in the war contributed to the misery of countless numbers of people I did not know and never saw. That emotional wound has scarred over, and I no longer lose much sleep over it.

Volunteer for Everything

Common advice military recruits receive is, "Don't volunteer for anything." I began ignoring that advice in basic training at Great Lakes. It became obvious to me early on that when some routine, repetitive chore needed doing, the person running the activity simply asked a question. "Who's from a small town?" People who raised their hands became volunteers.

We did everything as a company in boot camp, so when we went for a test or physical exam of one kind or another, all 120 of us went. Dental checkups included x-rays. That meant waiting your turn. One of the dental techs asked, "Has anyone here been to college?" I figured he needed help with a simple task of some kind. In a dental lab it certainly wouldn't involve heavy lifting. Up went my hand. For the next two hours while my mates squatted on the floor waiting their turn to get their teeth x-rayed, I worked in the darkroom developing film.

Another time, a couple of weeks into basic training, the captain asked, "Who can type?" Again, probably no heavy lifting. Up went my hand. That volunteer action got me out of the daily drudgery of learning how to march and doing pushups in the huge, dreary gym. Snow and ice made the grinder (marching field) too dangerous, so most of the physical training occurred indoors. Frostbite wasn't a concern, but the Navy didn't want anyone slipping on the ice and breaking a leg.

Each morning I reported to the cozy basement of an administrative building across the grinder from the barracks. A dozen recruits worked until quitting time typing letters to the families of the recruits. We typed short, generic messages like: "To: The Family of Navy Recruit John Doe: Your son, John, has been successfully inducted into the U.S. Navy and is currently in basic training at the Naval Training Facility in Great Lakes, Illinois." I typed dozens of those notes every day through two weeks of basic training.

My combined score in the English and math tests placed second highest in my company, a point below the top score. The tests didn't challenge me. I never learned what question(s) I missed. An eighth grader could have done the math. I had grammar at that level down cold. They either slipped in a trick question, or, THEY were wrong!

Something unexpected happened during basic training. We all got a few days of leave for Christmas. The personnel stationed at Great Lakes must have wanted to go home for the holiday. That's what I did. Sharon had graduated from Brookfield High School in 1968 and was attending Hannibal-LaGrange College in Hannibal, Missouri. She was home on semester break. Her family lived only a few blocks from the Stewart home.

Chapter 13

The Navy in Tennessee

After I completed basic training in February 1969, the Navy sent me to Naval Air Station Millington, Tennessee, for six months of electronics training. Millington is just northeast of Memphis. (My brother Scott had been through training at Millington a few years earlier).

One guy I befriended had his car on base, a Ford Mustang. We made a couple of road trips into Memphis to explore and get away from the Navy for a while. My twenty-first birthday arrived in April. Three of us rode the Mustang, in our whites, into Memphis so I could get my first legal drink in a bar. We spied a likely looking establishment named "Entrée Nous," or something very near that. It means "between us," but I had to look it up. I had taken French in college and recognized the language, so the name of the place caught my eye.

After being carded by the bartender we mounted barstools and ordered drinks. Tom Collins for me, my first drink in a bar as a 21-year-old!

A few people sat at tables scattered around the small lounge. Several couples huddled intimately. After a few minutes of sipping and looking around, one of the guys asked the bartender why there were no women in the bar. He leaned over and whispered, "This is a gay bar." We reacted quietly with a mixture of surprise, humor and embarrassment, paid our bill and swaggered out the door. This was 1969, long before gay people paraded in the streets.

My schooling in Millington didn't go well, mostly because the instructor spent most of class time telling jokes and Navy stories. Very little electronics instruction occurred, at least none that penetrated my brain. That turned out to be a blessing. Had I scored better, my training would have been extended, and I would have ended up working in an isolated shop repairing black boxes out of airplanes instead of replacing black boxes in airplanes. I wanted to be in and around the planes on the flight deck and hangar bay, not soldering tiny wires someplace in the bowels of a ship. My inability to understand the relationship of ohms, capacitors and sine waves served a purpose. The Navy made me an aviation fire control technician (AQ) instead of an aviation electronics technician (AE).

Another Unwise Decision

Once while stationed in Millington I got a weekend pass and caught a military cargo flight to the National Guard station at Lambert Field in St. Louis. From there I hitch-hiked toward home and Sharon in Brookfield. It didn't take long to get the driver of a big rig to stop for a sailor in uniform holding out his thumb on the shoulder of Interstate 70.

Getting to Columbia from St. Louis was the easy part. Getting to Brookfield proved more of a challenge. It took more than one willing driver. A couple of young girls heading north picked me up. They were going to Moberly, where my recruiter had met me several months earlier to take me to the Navy. When we got to Moberly, the girls dropped me off along Highway 63, in a snowstorm.

Little traffic interrupted the dark, and none of the drivers who did pass stopped to pick up a sailor standing beside the highway in a near blizzard. Fortunately, a motel shined in the night a quarter mile away. I lugged my bag to the motel, relieved to get out of the deluge. Brookfield remained fifty miserable miles away, and I didn't have enough money to get a room in the motel. I called Sharon. A couple of hours later I got rescued from the motel lobby by Sharon and her Dad, Jim. We didn't talk much on the drive back to Brookfield. Mr. Blankenship dropped me off at the Stewart house. Sharon told me later she cried and begged for thirty minutes before her Dad agreed to rescue me.

At the end of my leave I nagged someone into giving me a ride back to the St. Louis airport, where I caught a military shuttle from the Air National Guard terminal to Millington. That was my only hitch-hiking adventure out of Millington. Love makes you do courageously stupid things.

What's a Lemoore?

Millington trainees received postings at naval stations all around the world. Just as after basic training, few of us would ever see one another again. After a brief leave, I reported to Naval Air Station Lemoore in the San Joaquin Valley of California, forty miles south of Fresno and about two hundred miles from Los Angeles to the south and San Francisco to the north.

Before reporting to Lemoore, I spent several days of leave in Brookfield with my family and my fiancée. During that leave, Sharon and I sat in the Stewart living room and watched on television as Neil Armstrong took his "giant leap for mankind" onto the surface of the moon. It was July 20, 1969.

After more training, this time on the A7E Corsair II light bomber, the Navy assigned me to squadron VA-146 with the rank of AQ3, Aviation Fire Control Technician, Third Class. "V" is military shorthand for fixed-wing aircraft (as opposed to rotary wing, helicopter). "A" means attack, as opposed to "F" for fighter.

When fully loaded, VA-146 had about two hundred airmen and sixteen A7E Corsair IIs, light attack jet airplanes. When on Yankee Station, the Navy's name for the line of action in the Gulf of Tonkin, A7s dropped 500- and 1,000-pound bombs on the Ho Chi Min Trail and other targets in Vietnam.

On base I lived in a barracks with men from my squadron and others stationed at Lemoore. The open barracks were divided into spaces with four bunkbeds to a cubicle. We all shared the showers and bathroom in the center of the building.

Nearby were the PX where we bought personal items, the barbershop where they kept the floor clean by brushing clippings down your shirt, and the theater where we saw movies for a quarter. The most popular films thrilled us with brief flashes of female skin. Clint Eastwood in "A Fistful of Dollars" played at the base theater. I killed a few hours a week working out at the base gym. The officers' and the enlisted men's clubs where nearby. Mixed drinks cost a quarter, beer less.

Beets and Woodstock

Acres and acres of sugar beets separated the Lemoore airfield from the base housing area. The long rows of beets had shallow trenches between them. Throughout the day workers moved irrigation hoses from one trench to another. The valley got little rain. Gray school buses shuttled us the several miles to the airfield. Each of the squadrons worked a day shift and a night shift, and we carried on much as though we had regular civilian jobs.

In August 1969, while I became acquainted with the A7E jet, several dozen rock-and-rollers and a half million young people with shaggy hair and funky clothes converged on a farm in upstate New York. The three-day Woodstock Music Festival would go down in history as a seminal event, not just for music, but for the country.

Promoted as simply an outdoor concert, Woodstock grew into a peaceful protest of the Vietnam War. Many of the musicians who played there became famous. During his performance that closed the show, Jimi Hendrix blasted out his explosive guitar rendition of the *Star-Spangled Banner*. That recording has become an iconic reminder of the Woodstock festival, the Vietnam War and protests against it.

I have a copy of the four-record Woodstock album and still enjoy watching documentary films made of the event.

Super Bowl in the Hangar

On Sunday, January 11, 1970, I had afternoon watch duty in the hangar and the flight line outside the hangar. Sundays at Lemoore were like Sundays anywhere else. They were days off; we were closed. Watch duty involved walking around looking for fires and challenging infiltrators.

It was Super Bowl Sunday. My team, the Kansas City Chiefs, faced the Green Bay Packers in a repeat match-up of the first NFL vs. AFL championship game three years earlier. The Packers won that earlier game in Los Angeles.

Someone on duty in one of the shop offices in the hangar had the football game on a small television set that I could see through a window in the shop door. I lingered at the door for a couple of minutes every time my circuit took me past the shop. The Chiefs beat the Packers 23-7 in New Orleans. It put a spring in my step and a smile on my face through the end of my watch. (The Chiefs didn't return to the Super Bowl until fifty years later, in 2020, when they defeated the San Francisco 49ers 31-20 in Miami.)

Nevada Purgatory

Work at Lemoore focused on getting the squadron, its pilots and aircraft ready to go to war aboard an aircraft carrier. Before we deployed, the squadron moved itself and its equipment to Fallon, Nevada, to give the pilots a couple of weeks of training with their missile, bomb and cannon systems. Fallon, about fifty miles straight east of Reno, impressed me as a perfect place for a penal colony. Its primary natural resources are sand and scrub brush. After being in Fallon for two cold weeks, the prospect of nine months overseas didn't sound too inconvenient.

One particularly onerous task at Fallon involved landing watch duty. Me or another luckless rookie sat in a freezing little shack at the end of the runway for two hours at a time, far from civilization, and watched airplanes approaching to land. If a plane's landing gear wasn't down, the man on watch would fire a flare into the sky to alert the pilot. That never happened, of course. Like other activities, watch duty constituted little more than an exercise in military mind control. You don't have to like it, but you do what you're told. That's the bargain you enter when you take the oath.

CHAPTER 14

CARRIER QUALIFICATIONS

After the purgatory of Fallon, the squadron faced carrier qualifications, a four-week cruise aboard ship in preparation for the real thing. The personnel of VA-146 squadron flew to Guantanamo Bay Naval Base (Gitmo in military slang) on the southeastern tip of Cuba, to meet the U.S.S. America, CVA66.

The U.S. leased the forty-five square miles of Gitmo from Cuba in 1903. Since the Cuban Revolution of 1959, when Fidel Castro took power, the Cuban government has protested the presence of the U.S. military base, but the lease holds.

From the base, launches carried the men of VA-146 and their seabags out to the ship anchored in the bay. That was my first glimpse of an aircraft carrier. The America, at nearly eleven hundred feet long, didn't impress me from a couple of miles across open water. As our launch drew nearer, the carrier grew larger, then larger still until it loomed over our boat like a Great Dane eyeing a biscuit.

The America, commissioned in 1965, had a flight deck of about four and a half acres, a crew of nearly 3,000 sailors plus almost 2,500 airmen among the various squadrons aboard.

The USS America remained in service for more than thirty years. Then, after it sat rusting in Philadelphia for several years, the Navy towed the ship out to sea in May 2005. To help designers of the next generation of aircraft carriers, the Navy used the America to study damage caused by various types of explosions. The ship withstood four weeks of this abuse, then the Navy scuttled her off the east coast of the United States.

To Yankee Station

My first deployment, destination Yankee Station in the Gulf of Tonkin off the coast of Vietnam, took much of 1970, from April 10 to December 21. We would circle the globe. Leaving from the huge Naval base at Norfolk, Virginia, the America picked up the Air Wing in Mayport, Florida. It then sailed south, stopping at Rio de Janeiro, Brazil, before heading east across the Atlantic Ocean, around the Cape of Good Hope off South Africa, through the Indian Ocean to Subic Bay in the Philippines. From there the America joined the other ships on Yankee Station.

Just after leaving the United States, the America received word that it might have to rescue the Apollo 13 astronauts, whose lunar landing mission was cut short by an explosion on the spacecraft. As the landing on April 17 approached, it became apparent that Apollo 13 would splash down in the Pacific Ocean, and the America resumed its voyage across the Atlantic.

From Pollywog to Shellback

Sailors who have never crossed the equator at sea suffer the abuse of being called "pollywogs" by the "shellbacks," those who have crossed the 0-degree latitude line. As the ship crossed the equator, a messy initiation ceremony occured on the flight deck. Pollywogs crawled through a gauntlet of shellbacks who slapped their butts (gently, mostly) with chunks of old fire hose. Among other humiliations, pollywogs had to crawl up to a fat sailor sitting beside King Neptune with his bare belly covered in lard and gear grease. Each pollywog got his face rubbed on the belly before being anointed a shellback by the King.

In the spirit of the event, pollywogs are expected to go through this ritual voluntarily. I quietly abstained from the festivities. Acting like a ship photographer and avoiding anyone who would know of my pollywog status, I took my camera up to the flight deck and took pictures of the proceedings.

A shellback administers an initiation swat to a pollywog's backside during the traditional crossing-the-Equator ceremony.

Galley Duty

Daily flight operations in the Gulf of Tonkin lasted twelve hours, and usually occurred in the daylight, for obvious reasons. It's easier to spot targets and not get killed yourself when you don't have to depend entirely on instruments. But the flight deck of a carrier during flight ops offers many opportunities to get killed, even in daylight. Darkness compounds the hazards.

Training and constant focus on the moment prevent accidents. I worked the shift when the planes weren't flying. My ego likes to think the shop chief recognized me as a superior technician who should not be exposed to the dangers of flight operations. Supporting that theory is the fact that the chief sent me to work in the ship's galley for three months during the deployment. That virtually eliminated my exposure to danger.

Word had come down that the squadron needed to provide several people to transfer temporarily to the ship's crew. The AQ shop got tagged. Being the greenest member of the shop, the duty flowed to me. I moved from the squadron's birthing quarters to a ship's crew space.

The America had two dining rooms. The main dining room, aft, served full-course meals that changed from day-to-day. A smaller galley and dining room in a forward area served hamburgers, hot dogs and other light fare for those who didn't have time or didn't want to wait in line at the main dining room.

My job in the smaller dining area was to supervise a few of the ship's crew in keeping the tables, chairs and floors wiped off and mopped. Heavy duty. One of the knuckleheads on my crew kept me entertained with practical jokes like putting spoons and forks in the garbage disposal and turning it on. Funny stuff like that.

Sad News from Home

During the time I was reassigned to the ship's company, I received a letter from Mother informing me that William "Billy" Stewart of Sumner, my stepfather's father, had died.

In the mid-1960s I had the privilege of being in the blind with Billie on my first Canada goose hunt on the farm near Sumner. My brother Scott and a friend of his were also in the blind, which we had hunkered into before sunup on a frigid morning shrouded in low-hanging clouds. I was 16, armed with a .22 rifle/20-gauge shotgun over-and-under I had purchased at a sporting goods store on the square in Grinnell, Iowa. It cost $60, the same amount as my first car.

In those years, upwards of 400,000 Canada geese, "honkers" as locals called them, stopped on their southward migration at Swan Lake National Wildlife Refuge a mile south of Sumner. When they went out to feed each morning, the geese filled the sky over the countryside. Massive flocks in their familiar V formations poured over the fields looking for corn that had escaped the harvester. At least two dozen hunters hunkered in blinds spread across a field east of the Stewart farmhouse. At thirty minutes before sunrise, official shooting time, volley after volley of shotgun blasts roared from every direction, near and far. Geese rained out of the sky.

I accounted for none of the downpour. My gun held only one shot compared to the three shells in the automatic shotguns carried by virtually every other hunter in the field. A lone goose flew over, a bit high but in range. Boom-boom-boom roared the big guns from the others in the blind, followed a fraction of a second later by the "pop" of my little gun. The goose, which by then had reached the limit of shotgun range, tumbled to the earth. After all of the exclamations of "nice shot" and expressions of disbelief subsided, I ran across the stubble of the corn field to retrieve my honker. A single pellet from my shot had hit the underside of the goose's chin. It was the only wound on the bird.

On a great opening day of goose hunting, my miraculous shot got as much mention as anyone else's story around the kitchen table in the Stewart house. Scott's friend still remembers that shot. He had fired three times at the goose before I pulled my trigger.

The friend was the guy on my Little League team who had terrorized batters back in Grundy Center.

Chapter 15

"Gripes"

A "gripe" board atop the chief's desk leaned against the bulkhead in our small AQ shop one level below the flight deck. Gripes were problems with the airplanes. Gripes involving a weapons delivery system came to the AQ shop. A problem might be as simple as a bomb rack not receiving its signal from the cockpit to more complicated navigation or bomb trajectory issues.

Pilots reported gripes when they landed after sorties. Problems were written on red or green index cards that were inserted into the plane's sleeve on the gripe board. Red cards meant the plane could not fly again until the problem got fixed. Green cards meant the plane could fly missions, but something didn't work correctly.

Also among the squadrons aboard ship were a couple of A6 Intruder and two F4 Phantom outfits. F4s provided air cover for the bombers, keeping the enemy's MiGs at bay. Several helicopters and reconnaissance airplanes completed a carrier's total of about eighty aircraft.

It takes many manhours of maintenance for every hour a carrier-based warplane flies. The violent pounding of catapult launches and cable landings jars stuff lose. A7Es were among the sweethearts of the air wing because of their low ratio of maintenance hours to flight hours.

An F4 Phantom roars off of a port catapult as A7s line up for launch off the two bow cats.

Flight Operations

The carrier's island, which houses the crew and equipment directing flight operations, has several observation decks. They provide good vantage points, but they don't offer a complete picture of the violence involved with launching and recovering aircraft. The experience one deck below the flight deck adds another dimension. There you can feel the roar of the jet engines with their afterburners at full throttle just before launch. The ship shudders as a catapult slams the end of its channel and flings its load out over the ocean.

Landings serve up their own version of mayhem. When the tailhook of a plane snags a steal cable a breathtaking shriek penetrates the upper decks of the ship. The pilot pours on the power as the plane hits the deck in case the hook misses all four cables, which happens rarely. If it does happen, the plane shoots off the front of the ship and circles around for another landing attempt.

A dozen ways to die or to cause death lurk on the deck during the organized mayhem of flight ops. I can't imagine what flight operations would be like if the ship were under attack at the same time. If you're working in that chaos, you better be paying attention every second. Eighteen-to-22-year-olds under the direction of slightly older hands coordinate much of the action. With my habit of thinking about things other than what I'm doing, the flight deck during operations was no place for me.

Black Boxes

We worked in two-man teams during the off-ops shift. To power-up the electrical system on a plane, we unspooled a thick electrical cable from the edge of the flight deck or hangar deck and plugged it into the aircraft. "Black boxes" contain the circuits that operate systems on the plane and the cockpit instruments. After several weeks of flight operations we became good at determining quickly which black box needed to be changed to fix a gripe.

AQs worked on the plane's weapons delivery systems, from bombs to rockets to canons. A7Es had 30mm gatling guns that fired through an opening in the fuselage. Sidewinder air-to-air missiles attached to racks on the sides of the fuselage. Bombs hung in clusters on racks attached to pylons under the wings.

Black boxes that we changed out included the heads-up display unit (HUD), which earlier versions of the A7 did not have. The HUD unit went in the cockpit in the pilot's line of sight. The HUD control box and an 80-pound computer nestled beside each other in the left side of the plane under the leading edge of the wing. Hinged panels with quick-release latches gave access to several black boxes. If a pilot readying for takeoff noticed a problem, a technician often could replace a black box and resolve the issue in time for the pilot to make his launch.

We sometimes scavenged parts from a "hangar queen" to get a bomber back into action. Most squadrons had at least one hangar queen. They were planes with red gripes that nobody had been able to fix, not even the onboard civilian tech reps from the company that built the planes. Hangar queens weren't getting into action anytime soon, so their parts were fair game.

The War at Home

Back home, demonstrations against the war, especially on college campuses, made the news every day. Students rallied in the streets and occupied campus administration buildings. At the University of Missouri in Columbia, where I would attend after the Navy, students camped out in a park on a corner of the campus. The university later renamed the area Peace Park. I drove past it every day for twenty-five years on my way to work at the Missouri Press Association office.

The America had a daily news sheet of several pages with a few stories from back home, notes about the ship's schedule and a couple of cartoons. One day the paper had a story about the May 4 killings by National Guard troops of four students in an antiwar rally at Kent State University in Ohio. "What the hell is going on back home," I wondered.

Radar Antennas Don't Float

AQs also worked on the A7E's forward-looking radar. The radar's dish antenna sweeps back-and-forth inside the dome just above the gaping mouth of the engine intake. Once while working with a guy other than my usual teammate, we replaced the antenna on a plane. The other guy was carrying the antenna we had removed from a plane back to the shop. As we left the flight deck and stepped down the catwalk steps, he pitched the antenna over the railing into the sea sixty feet below. All I could say was, "What the ..." He just shrugged and went on to the shop.

An A7E belonging to the "World Famous" VA-146 Blue Diamonds on the flight deck of the U.S.S. America. All of the squadrons were "world famous" for some reason, although I had never heard of any of them before enlisting.

Bombs Appear, Disappear

This WestPac (Western Pacific) deployment of the America introduced the A7E to Yankee Station.

As my work shift progressed, pockets of space on the flight deck became increasingly more cluttered with loaded bomb carts as the red-shirted ordnance crews prepared for the next round of flight operations. On this deployment, VA-146's AQ shop where I worked occupied a small area directly below the island, the flight operations control center on the starboard side of the flight deck. The deck area around the island served as a staging area for the bomb racks. As we worked through the night going back and forth between the shop and our planes on the flight deck, finding a path among the racks of 500- and 1,000-pound bombs became trickier. By the end of the shift, we almost had to climb over bombs. When I arrived for my next shift after twelve hours of flight operations, all those bombs were gone.

Two squadrons of A7E Corsair IIs and two of A6 Intruders can deliver lots of bombs in twelve hours.

Heavy Music Loses Weight

The world of heavy music lost a lot of weight toward the end of 1970. Jimi Hendrix, the final performer at the Woodstock music festival the previous summer, died of a drug overdose on September 18. About three weeks later, on October 4, Janis Joplin overdosed.

Teeing it Up

My running mate during the America deployment and I played golf several times on the base at Subic Bay in the Philippines. Both of us had fiancés waiting for us at home, so we seldom ventured into the notorious Olongapo City just outside the main gate of the naval base. Olongapo, a colorful dump of a town, serviced the base. It provided several tightly packed blocks of dark saloons filled with women, ramshackle hotels with rent-by-the-hour rooms and take-out food stands. If you were looking for a wild time, you didn't have to look long or far in Olongapo.

At that time, sailors on shore had to wear their uniforms. Navy uniforms were not designed for golf. Besides looking strange on the links, they provide little give where you need it to play golf. The Navy removed the uniform regulation before my second deployment. Then we wore civilian clothes ashore.

Everyone who played golf at Subic Bay had to have a Philippine caddie. The course required a caddy fee of three dollars, no more or no less, for eighteen holes (we always paid more). Nobody rode a golf cart. We usually got the same caddies, who argued their way to the front of the caddie que when they saw us coming. Those men did a great job carrying our clubs and finding the balls we hit into the rough. Also, our poor play entertained them.

The tee box of the second hole on the golf course sat atop a steep hill. We grabbed onto a rope strung on a motorized pulley that hauled us up the trail through the jungle to the tee box. Driving off that tee was my favorite shot on the course. A well-hit ball carried over an expanse of wilderness to the fairway far below. The ball seemed to hang in the air forever. It sparkled in the sunshine against the deep green backdrop of the jungle.

Once as we approached a tee box a pack of monkeys emerged from the woods and ran us off. We waited a few minutes until the beasts melted back into the jungle. On another hole, a huge snake stretched out sunning on the green. We declared pars and moved on.

In August, the America visited Manila. The commander of the Seventh Fleet, Attack Carrier Strike Force, hosted Philippines President Ferdinand Marcos and his wife, Imelda, aboard ship. My friend and I, not having been invited to the formal festivities, went ashore and played a round of golf, in our whites.

Tonkin Gulf Yacht Club

Later in the deployment, the America participated in three separate exercises with naval units from China, Korea and Japan off the coast of Korea in the Sea of Japan. The America operated for one hundred days during five stints on Yankee Station.

Patrolling on Yankee Station qualified me to become a member of the unofficial Tonkin Gulf Yacht Club. No such outfit exists, as far as I know, but someone created a colorful round patch with those words on it and an oriental boat in the center. The colors of the patch, red stripes, black boat, border and lettering, and gold field, match the colors of the Vietnam service ribbon. I regretted not buying the patch while in the Navy. Many years later I found the patch among a display of hundreds in a military memorabilia shop in Branson, Missouri.

On the America's return toward home, heading east, the crew observed two Thanksgivings as the ship crossed the International Date Line on November 26.

Deep Water Swim Call

While cruising east of the Philippines the America passed over the Mariana Trench, at nearly seven miles the deepest trench on the earth. The captain issued a "swim call," a navy tradition when sailors are allowed to jump off the ship. With the ship drifting over the trench and Marines in launches to retrieve swimmers and watch for sharks, dozens of us jumped off one of the starboard aircraft elevators. With the elevator at its hangar bay position, we plunged about thirty feet into the Western Pacific.

During this deployment, the America made ports of call in Singapore, Manila, Sydney, Australia; and Japan. When entering a port, members of the crew, dressed in their whites or blues, depending on the season, stood at parade rest around the perimeter of the flight deck. Either the song "America" or the "Miss America" theme blasted from the flight deck speakers. At some of the ports the ship sat at anchor outside the harbor because the harbor could not accommodate a ship that size. In those ports launches took sailors to shore.

On the return home, we sailed across the South Pacific and around Cape Horn off the southern tip of South America. We stopped again in Rio before heading north to the America's home port at Norfolk, Virginia.

CHAPTER 16

CHILLY HONEYMOON

The America docked at Norfolk on December 21. A week later, on December 27, Sharon and I were married at the First Baptist Church just off the main square in Kirksville, Missouri. (Sharon's family had moved from Brookfield to Kirksville around 1968.) Sharon's two brothers and one of her two sisters, all of them younger than her, were in the wedding party, as were my two brothers, my sister Jackie and a cousin's child, who was the flower girl.

A couple of days before the wedding, I paid $1,100, virtually all the money I had saved, for a 1966 Plymouth Belvedere at a car lot in Brookfield. The dealer wouldn't budge on the price for the clean, baby-blue car.

For what perhaps could be called a honeymoon, Sharon and I drove to the wintery desolation of Iowa. We had little money and less time, where could we go? We spent our wedding night in a motel trending toward seedy in Ottumwa, Iowa. We visited the Ford family in Grinnell for a day, then I took Sharon to Grundy Center to show her the houses I grew up in.

When I went back to the Navy only days after getting married, I left the car with Sharon. She was attending Missouri Baptist Hospital School of Nursing in St. Louis, where she finished classes in the spring of 1971.

Several weeks after I got back to Lemoore, I received a phone call from Sharon. She had suffered severe bumps and bruises in a head-on collision on Highway 63 near Moberly. That news made me tremble, but she assured me she would be fine when the swelling went down and the bruises healed. She felt terrible about crashing the car. Her father had the Plymouth hauled to a body shop in Kirksville. The next time I saw the car it looked new.

Sharon and I in the Plymouth departing from the Kirksville church where we were married on December 27, 1970. I had just returned from deployment to the Gulf of Tonkin aboard the USS America. The Navy wanted me back in a week.

I attended Sharon's pinning ceremony in St. Louis after she completed studies for her nursing diploma. A month later, after Sharon took State Board exams, we rented a small U-Haul trailer, filled it with Sharon's clothes and our wedding gifts and drove west to Hanford, California, where we rented an apartment. I moved out of the barracks on the base, and we began living like regular people. I drove to the base each morning, and Sharon walked to work at the nearby Catholic hospital.

My Throat Gets Cut

Some days after Sharon and I settled at Hanford, I began to notice a minor pain and a visible lump in my throat. A doctor on the base at Lemoore determined that I needed surgery, and it couldn't wait. He suspected the lump might be cancer.

The surgeon at the base hospital removed a non-toxic thyroid tumor. The tumor may have been caused by the radiation treatment I had received as an infant in the hospital at Eldora, Iowa. While the tumor would not kill me, the procedure nearly did. The anesthesiologist gave me an overdose.

The timing of my medical situation didn't fit with the Navy's schedule. While I was in the hospital, my squadron left for its carrier qualification cruise in preparation for deployment to WestPac. The hospital discharged me after a couple of days, with orders to rest at home for two weeks. Cabin fever soon afflicted me, and I convinced Sharon that I could drive in to the shop on the base and sweep the floor or something. A bandage covered my throat, but I felt well.

Tweaking the Bombers

It didn't take long for the skeleton crew in the shop to see that I was fully functional. All of our airplanes were aboard the carrier Constellation off the California coast, so I had little to do. Somebody in charge soon thought of something I could do that turned out to be valuable to the squadron's mission. In preparation for deployment, airplanes need their weapons systems to be fine-tuned. This involved making sure all systems agreed on the location of a target and that any weapon deployed–bomb, missile or bullet–would strike the target. Navigation, targeting and weapon release systems had to be synchronized.

One at a time during the next two weeks, my squadron's A7Es were flown from the Constellation off the coast of California to the hangar at Lemoore. I mounted a large metal-framed instrument to the front of the planes. With it and other tools, I sighted the plane's canon and adjusted its other weapons delivery instruments.

Another procedure involved moving the planes to the compass rose out near the runway. A compass rose is a circular graphic etched into the concrete with compass directions on it. One wheel of the aircraft is anchored on a pivoting plate at the center of the compass. A pilot jockeys the plane around the rose, stopping on major directional points so the navigation instruments in the cockpit can be adjusted to match the actual magnetic coordinates of the earth.

A pilot in the cockpit and a crewman on the ground communicate numbers one through ten quickly with one hand. Two fingers pointing up means the number two. Two fingers pointing horizontally means seven–five plus two. Tweaks to navigational systems were completed quickly.

When the squadron returned from carrier qualification, some of my mates asked how I'd enjoyed my vacation. Most hadn't missed me. I vaguely remember the company commander issuing a letter of commendation for my work while I was medically authorized to be off duty. If he did, I lost it. Maybe my imagination conjured the letter.

Shocking Development

I got the shock of my life while working on one of the airplanes in the hangar. It reminded me of the jolt I received in the basement of our house in Grundy Center. The plane had just arrived from the Constellation for my adjustment of its weapons systems. When I reached up to open the radome (radar dome), a tiny bolt of electricity shot into my little finger and down my arm. I howled and hopped around the hangar shaking my hand for several minutes. My finger felt like it had a needle sticking in it for the rest of the day.

Other sailors were experiencing similar shocks when working on their A7s. The friction of a flying plane builds up a powerful charge of static electricity on the body of the craft. Planes have devices attached to bleed off the static. What's left of the electricity discharges through the tires when they touch ground.

Somehow, radomes on A7Es were losing connection to the body of the planes, so the static buildup on the radomes was not discharging. The Navy resolved the problem with a quick, interim fix. It had short cables installed between the bodies of the aircraft and their radomes. Until the fix, we used a screwdriver with a cable attached to it to discharge any static electricity on the radome. A crude but effective jerry rig for a modern, multimillion-dollar warplane.

Bumped Up

Before the squadron deployed for WestPac, I passed the written test to become a petty officer, second class, a pay rating of E-5. I thought I had failed miserably; maybe even be stripped of my one "crow" as an AQ Third Class. Sailors in their first enlistment had no chance to advance beyond E5. Apparently, the enlistments of many AQ2s had expired, and the Navy needed to replenish the ranks.

The insignia for the rank and rating (job title) is an eagle (commonly called a "crow") over two V stripes. The aviation fire control technician (AQ) insignia, which rides above the stripes on the patch, is a scope mounted on a winged tripod. A few years after my service, AQs ceased to exist when the Navy combined them with other ratings into the aviation electronics technician (AT) designation.

Chapter 17

Aboard the "Connie"

My second deployment, aboard the USS Constellation, began October 1, 1971. The "Connie" left its home port of San Diego, stopped for a couple of days in Pearl Harbor, Hawaii, then proceeded to Subic Bay, where it made final preparations for duty on Yankee Station in the Gulf of Tonkin.

The VA-146 AQ shop aboard the Constellation occupied a small space on the port side one level below the flight deck and two above the hangar deck. On the carrier America during the previous deployment, the squadron worked out of a shop on the opposite side of the ship.

One night I was working alone on a plane tied down on the flight deck at the bow. The gripe involved the plane's radar, so I had an aluminum ladder with me to open the radome on the front of the plane to get to its antenna. While I was working, the officer in charge came on the flight deck loudspeaker and announced the approach of a heavy squall. He warned all personnel to get off the flight deck as soon as possible.

Either the officer didn't give early enough warning, or I lingered too long. The squall caught me up the ladder. By the time I climbed down, I was under assault by torrents of rain coming sideways in the wind, with the ladder flapping in my hand. A sailor on watch on the flight deck saw my distress. He helped get me and the ladder out of the raging storm.

One routine chore of the AQ shop involved checking the bomb release circuits of every plane before flight ops. This involved a simple light test to make sure the signal from the joystick in the cockpit reached the bomb rack. When a plane takes off from a carrier with bombs hanging under its wings, you don't want that plane carrying any of those bombs when it comes back and lands. Whether or not the planes had any targets, those bombs were going to be dropped, onto a target or into the jungle or ocean.

Spectacular Skies

Being at sea offers spectacular views of the night sky. Small red lights atop the flight deck's island are the only illumination up top on the carrier. With a bright moon, we needed flashlights with red lenses, which preserved our night vision, only for close work. The moon provided enough light for many routine tasks.

When there was no moon, the Milky Way took my breath away. Our galaxy presents as a vast ribbon of light, the view toward its edge, stretching from horizon to horizon. As an urban dweller, I miss that spectacle. Even minor light pollution from the ground dilutes the splendor of the Milky Way. Sometimes, when traveling through the dark countryside during winter, when the air is clear and crisp and no moon obscures the brilliance of the other objects in the sky, I pull off the road to refresh my memory of Earth's awesome ceiling.

The officer of the day clicked on the ship's intercom one night and told us of an electrical storm several miles astern off the port side. I went up to the flight deck for a look. In the distance, flash after flash of lightning crackled continuously among the boiling clouds of that fiercely magnificent storm. The thunder died before it reached us.

One night we didn't have much to keep us busy. I had finished working on an aircraft on the flight deck and lingered up there gazing at the sky. I was lying on my back with my head resting on the tow bar of a plane. Apparently, concerned that I had not returned to the shop, our chief petty officer, a surly career man (lifer), came looking for me. I didn't see him coming. He kicked my foot and hissed, "Get back to the shop!"

Months later, when I returned to work after a post-deployment leave, I learned that our chief had got drunk and killed an elderly couple and himself in a head-on collision. I mourned the elderly couple.

Wings of Hope

Sometimes the most insignificant occurrence can flip your mood instantly. That happened to me one day when I was leaving my shift in the AQ shop. We worked twelve-hour shifts. As usual, I worked the shift opposite flight operations. My shift fixed gripes that developed on the planes as they delivered bombs during flight ops. We got the birds ready for the next round of sorties while the flight ops crew rested up.

The Connie had been on Yankee Station for a couple of weeks delivering bombs inland every day. That meant I worked at night. After a shift in the artificial light at night, just a hint of natural light in the eastern sky shot painful needles into my eyes. Those needles had me squinting as I left the shop to get some breakfast before heading to my bunk for some sleep. Sometimes I got too hungry to sleep and too tired to eat, a dilemma. Eating usually came first, but not always.

Flight operations spread a greasy film over the flight deck, the hangar deck and what seems like everything in the decks between them. Exhaust from the jets and the ship and the residue of tires after hundreds of launches and recoveries turns everything greasy and gray in the humid ocean air.

This gloomy atmosphere turned my mood greasy and gray as well. My countenance, even my trudging gate, reflected this dour state. I felt basted in the same sticky residue as the deck. I proceeded across the hangar bay toward the aft galley, ducking bomb pylons under aircraft wings and stepping over tie-down cables.

Then it happened. A monarch butterfly appeared flitting about between two of our bombers. My mouth dropped open as I watched the monarch zig-zag around like butterflies do. It rose up and danced its jig over the top of one of the planes and out of sight.

The incongruity of that butterfly being in the hangar bay of a warship at sea transported me. I shed my gloom like a snake slithering out of old skin. A grin lit my face; a bounce entered my stride. Seeing that butterfly for only a few seconds had blasted me out of a deep funk. It felt physical. It reminded me of the beauty in the world and the good things in my life, and that I would return to them soon. How long that emotional euphoria lasted I don't recall, but I remember it vividly.

Top Guns

Something of significance to military historians and to the Constellation occurred early in May 1972, near the end of the deployment. Typical for the time, the Air Wing aboard the Connie included two squadrons of F4 Phantoms, the workhorse fighter jet of the Navy in those years. F4s carried two people, the pilot and the navigator, and their mission involved protecting the bombers on their sorties over Vietnam.

Lt. Randy Cunningham and Lt. JG (junior grade) Willie Driscoll, flying an F4 off the Connie, shot down three MiGs in a dogfight over North Vietnam. With the two MiGs the pair had shot down on previous sorties, they became the first aces (five enemy planes shot down) of the Vietnam War.

The ship held a brief celebration for its new celebrities.

Hong Kong Hurricane

The Constellation anchored outside Hong Kong harbor for a scheduled week away from Yankee Station. A number of Navy wives, Sharon among them, chartered a plane and flew to the city at the southeastern tip of China.

At that time, 1972, Great Britain controlled Hong Kong. The colony reverted to Chinese control in 1997.

Sharon and I enjoyed listening to this woman singing in the piano bar of the Hong Kong Hilton Hotel.

Sharon and I stayed at the Hong Kong Hilton. One evening we went to the hotel lounge and listened to a southeast Asian woman singing beside the piano. Some weeks later, when the Constellation visited Singapore, I went into the lounge of the Hilton Hotel there. Singing at the piano was the same woman Sharon and I had enjoyed listening to in Hong Kong.

Mother Nature cut short our visit to Hong Kong. A hurricane bore down on the coastal city, and the Navy ordered the Constellation to sea to avoid the storm. The wives remained in Hong Kong for another couple of days before flying back to California, but our rendezvous was over.

Secret Shipmates

Twenty years later, when I was working for the Missouri Press Association, I went to Lebanon, Missouri, to interview the newspaper publisher there. He had been elected president of the National Newspaper Association. We needed a feature story about him for *Missouri Press News* magazine, the monthly publication that I produced as editor.

A small model of an A6 Intruder sat on the publisher's desk. I asked him about it. The publisher had served in the Navy, flying A6s. He still flew helicopters in the Reserves.

We chatted about our Navy service and soon discovered that we had been on the Constellation together. He remembered visiting Hong Kong, where he also stayed at the Hilton Hotel. He didn't leave when the ship did, though. He said he returned to the hotel, walked into the lobby and heard that the Constellation had been ordered to sea because of the approaching hurricane. He turned around and walked back out. How he managed to avoid trouble for missing the ship, I don't know.

I didn't get in trouble either, when I missed the ship a little while later.

Chapter 18

Adventure in Japan

Most sailors who served aboard carriers during the Vietnam War didn't receive combat action ribbons. My friend George and I did get those ribbons, but we had to go AWOL to do it. The two of us had become friends over our mutual interest in taking pictures. Like me, George was an AQ, aviation fire control technician. George worked during flight operations; I worked the twelve-hour shift between flight operations.

This story in no way intends to tarnish the shine of a combat action ribbon. Combat action is serious. Anyone who has endured combat in service to the country deserves a ribbon, at the very least.

George, an eager, adventurous young man from Pennsylvania, and I had been deployed on the Constellation for about eight months. Now the ship was headed home. On the way it docked in Yokosuka, Japan, for several days off-loading war-making equipment and on-loading boxes and crates full of stereo components, motorcycles and other items sailors had purchased during the deployment. Among the treasurers were two Japanese bicycles – Silk Cycles – I bought for Sharon and me.

George and I had purchased 35mm cameras from the PX at Subic Bay in the Philippines. Ships patrolling Yankee Station in the Gulf of Tonkin often visited Subic Bay, site of a major naval station, for supplies and liberty. Although United States ships continue to use Subic Bay, the Philippines took over administration of the base years ago.

Tokyo Tourists

While the ship was in Yokosuka preparing to cross the Pacific Ocean for home, George and I decided we needed to visit Tokyo, about fifty miles to the north. To get permission for such an excursion, we filled out a chit requesting a couple of days off. The chit needed to tell where we would stay and provide a phone number where we could be reached. George and I had no idea where we would end up. We had no hotel or phone number to write on the chit. A solution quickly presented itself.

Stacks of boxes containing record turntables, amplifiers and speakers cramped our shop aboard ship. Many guys, including me, took advantage of the low prices at military base stores to buy stereo equipment. Printed on the stacked boxes were the names of the manufacturers of the contents. One box had this stamped on it: Matsushita Corp.

On the chit requesting a pass I wrote Matsushita Hotel, Tokyo, and a random phone number. What shop chief would deny a pass to a couple of hard-working squids who'd been away from home for eight months? Some chiefs might, ours didn't.

With the Constellation not scheduled to leave for a few more days, off we went, George and I. By train. In Japan, walk or take a cab to a nearby train station, and in a few minutes you can be on your way to almost anywhere in the country you care to go.

It was springtime, the Easter season to be more precise. Warm, sweet air and bright sunshine compelled people into the streets. Many citizens exhibited something close to giddiness, cabin fever broken. The Japanese were not involved in our military unpleasantness to the south, other than profiting mightily from the military traffic, and they were shrugging off winter with gusto. George and I explored a bit of Tokyo and enjoyed watching adults playing with their laughing children. Masses of cherry blossoms splashed the city with pink. We ascended to the observation deck of Tokyo Tower, which a marquee proclaimed is a replica of the Eiffel Tower in Paris, but built with much less steel, a "superior" Japanese product.

Bad Wallbangers

Late in the afternoon, we found a hotel adjacent to a small urban lake bordered by cherry trees. We checked out the lounge in the hotel. At that early hour not even a bartender lurked there. When we finally attracted someone's attention, George and I ordered Harvey wallbangers, a popular cocktail at the time. The bartender had never heard of it. A Harvey wallbanger contains vodka and orange juice, like a screwdriver, and Galliano, a sweet herbal liqueur. The Galliano, added last, floats on top. The bar did have Galliano, in a thin bottle about three feet tall, but strange as it sounds, it had no orange juice. The bartender used Tang. I haven't had a Harvey wallbanger since. Tang nourishes astronauts, but it makes a foul wallbanger.

The next morning, full of excitement to begin the voyage home, George and I caught a southbound train. We headed back to the Navy with rolls of film to send off for developing.

American Pie

Before reaching Yokosuka, George and I decided to get off the train at Kamakura, a colorful city just north of Yokosuka. A brief walking tour of the neighborhood around the train station made us thirsty. A sign over a door in the front of a building brought us to a halt. It looked like it might be a lounge where a person could order a cocktail. In we went.

Calling it a lounge assigns it too much class. The hole-in-the-wall bar, dim and smoky, fell in size a bit shy of the average one-car garage. A horseshoe bar encroached on it entirely. Four or five patrons occupied the perimeter. George and I bellied up among them.

A young man ran the show, arms and hands flying about behind the bar like an orchestra conductor. His cigarette lighter appeared instantly out of nowhere. This trick repeated itself every minute or two as one or another of the barflies reached for a smoke. The bartender mixed drinks while leaning across the bar to light cigarettes.

George and I lingered only briefly, but my memory of that no-account dive sticks with me for two reasons. That bartender had a fresh drink in front of a customer before the empty glass hit the bar and a light for his cigarette before it was tapped out of the pack. Regardless of what it is, work done well impresses me. I'm sure I responded with a healthy tip, which was of course the reason for the bartender's alacrity.

A song is the second reason for the memory. A jukebox in a corner of the bar played *American Pie* repeatedly all the time George and I sat there. Among the few people in the bar, I suspect only George and I understood the lyrics. Not until I wrote this did it dawn on me that the handful of natives in the bar played *American Pie* time after time only because George and I were there. Until now, I just assumed they liked the tune. I did. My skull at times like this appears thick and hunkers low on my neck. Things don't penetrate; they fly right over. Maybe those Japanese barflies were serenading us. Or mocking? I'll never know. By not engaging, we had missed a chance to advance international relations, or set them back a bit.

Thirst quenched, George and I caught the train to Yokosuka.

We Visit the Shore Patrol

We caught a cab at the train station and told the driver, "Take us to the Constellation."

"Connie gone," said the driver.

"The Constellation can't be gone. It's not supposed to leave until tomorrow."

"Connie gone," the cabby repeated.

We told him to take us anyway. He shrugged and drove to the pier where the Connie indeed, was gone. George and I had missed movement.

"Take us to the Shore Patrol," I told the cabby. A few minutes later we found ourselves in the lobby of the Shore Patrol station with sixteen other sailors who had missed the Constellation. We probably weren't that cab driver's first Connie fares that day.

In the military, if your outfit goes someplace, and you don't go with it, you've "missed movement." You're not supposed to miss movement. Once upon a time, sailors got hung from the yardarm for missing movement. I started imagining what a brig looked like from the inside.

Not knowing what to do with this crew of malingerers, the Shore Patrol person in charge put us to work in the area. Someone gave me a rickety leaf rake and told me to spruce up the grounds around a nearby administration building. There wasn't a leaf in sight. I hadn't been scratching around in the dirt for half an hour when someone hollered at me.

All of us delinquents were hustled onto a Navy harbor launch and ferried out to the USS Albert David, a destroyer escort anchored in the harbor. Like the Constellation, the Albert David had been on its way home. The Navy called it back to Yankee Station in response to an invasion of South Vietnam by the Viet Cong and North Vietnamese. That invasion became known as the Easter (or Spring) Offensive.

Chapter 19

Back to the War

A t anchor, the Albert David's crew of fewer than two hundred rearmed and resupplied to head back to the war. Its guns had been removed for the trip across the Pacific Ocean. Cranes hoisted them back aboard. George and I and the other Constellation sailors clambered aboard what looked to me like a miniature ship. The eighteen Connie swabbies swelled the Albert David's crew by about twenty percent.

We became adjunct crewmen aboard the Albert David. While we were under way, a supply helicopter delivered gun supplies. All of us AWOLs joined the ship's crew in a human conveyor system. We walked around the perimeter of the ship's main deck, a circuit considerably shorter than a lap around a basketball court. As we passed a stack of ordnance on the stern, each of us accepted a gunpowder charge or a five-inch diameter shell and carried it to sailors stocking the magazine near the bow.

In the following days, the Albert David patrolled the shoreline of Vietnam in the Gulf of Tonkin. Once a small boat came alongside and a brief exchange occurred between a man on the boat and an officer on the Albert David. George and I speculated that our ship had been given coordinates of targets on land.

During general quarters, when the crew manned battle stations, the Albert David fired its guns. Not being members of the regular crew, we did not have battle stations, so we stayed out of the way. We donned life jackets and sprawled on the floor in the main passageway that ran through the ship.

Even the ship's small guns jolted the Albert David as the powder bags detonated and flung shells into the jungles or rice paddies of Vietnam. During at least one of these actions, the Albert David drew return fire. Holes in the ship's flag indicated the accuracy of the enemy gunners.

Members of the VA-146 Fire Control Technician crew in their shop aboard the Constellation. I'm standing in the doorway. I'm blurred more than the others because I didn't get settled before the camera timer went off. My "missed movement" partner, George Swanger, is seated in the center.

This Ship Rocks!

Destroyer escorts, at shorter than three hundred feet, lack the impressive size of an aircraft carrier or battleship. What they lack in size, they make up for in discomfort. Aboard the Albert David I learned to sleep on my back with my legs and arms spread to the edges of the bunk to keep from rolling onto the deck.

Unlike the Constellation, which responded sluggishly and almost imperceptibly to ocean swells, the Albert David rolled and pitched like a drunk on a skateboard. During my ten days of service on the Albert David, my bowels seized up, causing missed movements of another sort. The struggle to remain seated while the ship rolled and pitched discouraged relaxation.

While on the Albert David I became a fan of blues singer Nina Simone. Someone in the bunk room had a Simone tape. I borrowed it and played it repeatedly during the many hours with little more to do than read, which I did for hours.

The USS Albert David tied up to a pier at Guam. After riding on an aircraft carrier, a few days aboard this destroyer escort gave me a taste of another side of the Navy. A carrier patrols the ocean waves like a massive iceberg. This ship rides atop them like a cork.

Gassing Up in Guam

One miserably hot day, after the Albert David had been relieved of duty on Yankee Station, the ship docked in Guam for several hours to take on fuel. Guam, in the Pacific Ocean, is well east of Vietnam.

Just off the pier, a stack of cased beer the size of a family sedan sat cooking in the sun beside a small picnic-type shelter in a dusty, parched field. The mountain of beer looked as if it remained there permanently for crewmen of ships stopping here for supplies. A few of the guys attempted to play ball in the heat and choke down hot beer. Most of us just lounged with our tongues hanging out in any patch of shade we could find.

I was never so glad to get back aboard ship as when we departed Guam for the trip across the Pacific Ocean. Anyone who dreams of spending time relaxing on an exotic South Pacific island needs to understand this: It gets hotter than you can imagine.

Shuttle Service

After bobbing around on the Albert David for a week and a half, the sailors from the Constellation, one-by-one, slipped into a harness dangling beneath a helicopter hovering over the aft deck. The chopper hoisted us into its hold and deposited us on the aft deck of a nearby supply ship, the USS Mars. We were ushered into that ship's library, a hot place, where we sprawled on the floor in the corners and among the few tables and chairs.

George and I quickly determined that the cramped library just wouldn't do. Out we slipped in search of better accommodations. We found quiet, comfortable lodging in the captain's launch, which hung in its berth on deck. We were stowaways of sorts, after all.

The next day, George, the other prodigals and I boarded a helicopter that flew us to the Constellation, which by then was on its way home. The first question we got from our squadron mates: "How was your leave in Japan?" That's where they thought we'd been. What they hoped to hear about was our miserable confinement in the brig for missing the ship's movement.

Getting back to the Constellation brought tremendous relief to me in more ways than one. Once again, we were bound for home, and I stopped missing movements.

For service in the line of fire aboard the Albert David – that's what my military records say – the Navy awarded Combat Action Ribbons to all eighteen of us prodigals. (The Navy didn't know how else to spin this embarrassment.) The citations amounted to letters in our records, not actual ribbons, which we had to buy. I didn't buy one; I hadn't earned it.

Under the Golden Gate

The Constellation anchored for a night outside San Francisco Bay, waiting for low tide so it could sail under the Golden Gate Bridge. We entered San Francisco Bay late in June, 1972. The ship off-loaded the Air Wing and proceeded to its port at San Diego. The deployment officially ended June 30.

George told me this story only recently. We were paid with U.S. Treasury checks when we reached San Francisco. George said he went into a Bank of America, but it would not cash his check because he did not have an account. George went into a bank across the street. "The lady teller welcomed me home, cashed my check and mentioned how much money I had," George said. "She said, 'Young man, don't get hit on your head and robbed.'"

Airmen of VA-146 and sister squadron VA-147 boarded buses for a rowdy trip home to Lemoore. My beautiful wife, Sharon, had driven our car to the base. She greeted me dressed in an eye-popping top and spectacular short-shorts. They were burgundy. A guy from my shop rode with us in the Plymouth to Hanford, a frustrating half-hour drive.

While I remained in the Navy until August, the end of the Constellation deployment effectively ended my useful service. I continued the daily commute from Hanford to the base at Lemoore, but any actual work I did amounted to no more than routine maintenance of our aircraft. Most of the flying amounted to the pilots logging hours, so the AQ shop had little to keep a short-timer occupied.

I had enrolled for the fall semester at the University of Missouri in Columbia and completed the paperwork to have the government send a monthly check to the university to pay my tuition. With those details attended to, the Navy discharged me in August 1972, three months before the official end of my four-year enlistment.

Chapter 20

Student Veteran

My journalism degree came courtesy of the federal government through the GI Bill. It paid $315 a month directly to the University of Missouri, covering tuition. Qualifying for GI Bill benefits was one of the reasons I had enlisted in the Navy in 1968. Later, Sharon and I bought our first house with a GI Bill mortgage that required no down payment.

Another benefit: One visit to a VA dentist for whatever I wanted done. This led me to a decision that should not have been made. My wisdom teeth weren't bothering me, but they might in the future, so I decided to have them removed. I went to the VA Hospital in Columbia where a dental surgeon with thick glasses and belly climbed onto my chest, broke up my wisdom teeth and yanked them out. I laid around our apartment moaning and groaning and bleeding for several days. The numbness in the back of my gums didn't subside for years. My allergy to codeine revealed itself during the dental surgery debacle. I inherited that allergy from my mother.

Sharon and I lived in a complex called Broadmoor Apartments on the southeast corner of Stadium Boulevard and West Ash Street in Columbia. The name of the complex has changed, but the buildings look the same as they did forty-five years ago. When the weather permitted, I rode my Japanese Silk Cycle to campus. Sharon worked at Rusk Rehabilitation Center, which at that time abutted University Hospital three miles down Stadium from our apartment. We still had the 1966 Plymouth. Sharon drove it to work.

The University gave me credit for history and literature correspondence courses I had taken while in the Navy, but it still took me two fall semesters, two spring semesters, plus classes taken during two summer terms, to complete requirements for my Bachelor in Journalism degree. The university presented my diploma in the summer of 1974 during a mass Commencement. Students stood as a group when their school's turn came, and their dean offered congratulations. It may have been a bit more involved, but that's the gist.

My mother and stepdad, Donna and Bob Stewart, with me after the University of Missouri Commencement for the School of Journalism, Class of 1974.

Getting a Real Job

Now I had to find work. Responses came from several of the resumes I mailed out. Most simply stated they had no openings. Except for one, they were straightforward but polite. Along with my resume I had sent snapshots of myself. This was 1974. My photo showed a young man with a partial beard who needed a haircut, a common look at that time, especially for graduates of journalism school.

A publisher from Iowa wrote that no way in the world would he hire "a damned hippy" to work at his newspaper. My presumption to apply for a job with his publication insulted him. I wondered what kind of stuffy newspaper a rude person like that could publish? His letter topped the small packet of replies I received and kept for many years.

The newspaper in Poplar Bluff, Missouri, the *Daily American Republic*, needed a reporter. Would I come down for an interview? An opportunity! Sharon, three-months pregnant, and I drove the five hours from Columbia into the Southeast Missouri heat with the windows open on the Plymouth. Some cars of 1966 vintage had air conditioning. Ours didn't.

Poplar Bluff sits atop the Missouri bootheel, on the western edge of the Mississippi River bottomland and the east edge of the Ozark foothills.

The *Daily American Republic*, known locally as the *DAR*, published in the afternoon, Monday through Saturday, no paper on Sunday. The Wolpers and Stanard families had owned the newspaper for many years. John Stanard, the editor, leaned toward graduates of the Missouri School of Journalism, the first school of journalism in the world. John was a J School alum. I joined the *DAR* staff a few days after the interview.

Watergate Summer

The Watergate hearings occurred during our final months in Columbia. They focused on the fallout after a handful of men had been caught breaking into the offices of the Democratic National Committee in the Watergate hotel complex in Washington, D.C. Evidence pointed to people close to President Richard Nixon.

As the inquiry proceeded, attempts to shield people and mislead Congress pointed to Nixon himself. I watched many hours of the congressional hearings into the affair, which came to be called simply "Watergate."

The relentless work of *Washington Post* reporters Bob Woodward and Carl Bernstein, using tips from their unidentified source, called "Deep Throat," provided the momentum for the investigation. They wrote a book about their work titled "All the President's Men." Robert Redford played Woodward and Dustin Hoffman played Bernstein in the 1976 movie based on the book. The movie received eight Academy Award nominations and won four Oscars. "Rocky" beat it out for Best Picture.

Woodward and Bernstein's work also led to much discussion in my journalism classes at MU. "When is it appropriate to use confidential sources?" "How do you corroborate information received from a secret source?" "How far must you go to get a response from a person named in a story?" "What do you do when an official makes a statement that you know is false?"

Although Nixon declared, "I am not a crook," tape recordings of Oval Office conversations, which were secret until an aide made their existence known, indicated otherwise. As Congress moved toward impeaching Nixon, he resigned.

Sharon and I were in the car on our way to our new life in Poplar Bluff in a heavy downpour when we heard the news on the radio of Nixon's resignation. I smiled broadly through the furiously flapping windshield wipers. Two young, scruffy reporters had brought down a crooked president. "Finally, a win for the good guys," I thought.

CHAPTER 21

FIRE IN THE NIGHT

O nly a few weeks after I joined the *Daily American Republic*, the editor called me in the middle of the night. The radio scanner that he kept turned on at his home around the clock had awakened him. Fire crews were at a building downtown that had smoke coming out of it. "Check it out," Mr. Stanard said. The building, on one of the main intersections of downtown, held a hardware store. It sat across the street from the parking lot of the *Daily American Republic*. Sharon and I lived in an apartment not more than a mile from downtown, so it took only a few minutes for me to dress and drive to the scene.

Soon after I arrived and parked a couple of blocks away from the scene, four firemen entered the building through a rear basement door. No flames were visible, but smoke seeped out around window frames. Flashing lights on emergency vehicles splashed color across store buildings. Idling fire engines added a soundtrack to the eerie scene. I watched from the sidewalk across the street from the smoking building.

Bricks Litter the Street

Suddenly, a muffled explosion blew out the side of the structure, littering the street in front of me with bricks and debris. "Damn, we've got dead firemen!" I thought. Then, "I need to call the boss and get help." Unfortunately, the collapsing building had cut the electricity and telephone service in the area. Cell phones, indispensable now for news reporters, remained many years in the future. I had no way to call for help, and I did not want to leave the scene of the action to find a working phone.

I began making pictures. Bystanders and other firemen waded toward the now flaming building and dragged out what I thought were the bodies of firemen. Moments later, I heard to my left in the middle of the street a faint plea, "Help me, help me." As I looked toward the sound, a figure rose up slightly from the rubble in the street. Another fireman! Alive! He was on his hands and knees directly under overhead wires whipping violently as the conflagration convulsed the building.

Hoping to get a picture of bystanders dragging this fireman to safety, I looked around to shout for help. The street was deserted. Everyone who had been there was busy moving the other firemen or scrambling for more equipment to fight the fire.

That left me, standing there with a journalism school rule fresh in my brain: Record the news, don't become part of it. "To hell with that," I thought. "I'm the only one here!" Quickly stepping through the clutter of bricks, I reached the man and grabbed around an arm to help him up. This was a big man, dressed in firefighting gear.

Fortunately for both of us, another man hurried over. "This way," he said, and we helped the fireman stagger to the parking lot behind the newspaper office. We laid the fireman in the back of the man's pickup truck, and he drove to an emergency room three blocks away. The next day I learned that the man with the pickup truck was the father of the fireman we dragged out of the rubble. He had been sitting in his truck watching the action.

Fuzzy Photos

Meanwhile, the fire grew. It eventually engulfed several businesses before being contained. I spent the next couple of hours taking pictures, retrieving more film from the *DAR* darkroom and taking more pictures. (Like cell phones, digital cameras were years in the future. At the *DAR*, we spooled our own film from bulk, 100-foot rolls of black-and-while film.) One picture I hoped would be useable showed a fireman pouring gasoline from a five-gallon can into a pumper truck. To my utter horror and embarrassment, not a single nighttime picture I made of that fire was in sharp focus. The *DAR* printed several of them anyway.

When the rest of the newsroom staff arrived that morning, I wrote a first-person account of the fire. The newspaper went to press around noon. The collapse of the building had not killed a single fireman. One of them suffered a mangled leg, which had to be removed. The man I helped drag out of the bricks suffered a minor neck fracture.

The fire station already was part of my daily beat. Each morning I visited the station to check out calls made during the previous day. After the fire, smiles greeted me at the station every day. Before the fire, I was just the nosy reporter looking into their business. I had become a minor hero among those real ones.

Some months later the fire gained new life. The county prosecuting attorney called me at home on a Sunday evening. He asked me to come to his office the next morning. He said he was going to file arson charges in the fire that had destroyed the hardware store and other businesses. He wanted me to get the news first. That made me proud. I began to understand more clearly how important a local newspaper is to a community. Even when it seems nobody is paying attention, many are.

A Reporter's Playground

Through the years at the *DAR*, I moved from the fire/police/county beat to courts and the city administration. With the go-ahead from the editor, I started weekly pages dedicated to local business, outdoors and religion. Along with the routine coverage of the city and county, the region provided enough fires, robberies, drownings, crashes, floods, train derailments and homicides – a reporter's smorgasbord – to keep our staff hopping and happy. We wrote plenty of human-interest feature stories, too.

I filled in on the editor's desk a few times when Mr. Stanard took a break. On one of those occasions, in November 1978, a U.S. congressman was murdered and more than 900 members of a religious sect, many of them Americans, committed suicide in the South American country of Guyana. The people had drunk a flavored drink spiked with cyanide to escape what their leader told them was the evil world about to descend upon them. Investigators determined that many of the people who died had been forced to drink the poison. That tragedy led to the phrase "drank the Kool-Aid" to describe acceptance of ideology without question or basis in fact. (Most official reports of the event indicated the flavored drink to be a different brand than Kool-Aid.) *Editor & Publisher* magazine used my front-page layout of the AP photos and account of that horrible incident in an article about how to present a multi-piece story.

Mob Scene

One summer several hundred area farmers blocked the main intersection in Poplar Bluff, where Highway 60 joined Highway 67. The cost of diesel fuel ranked high among their complaints. To emphasize their point, dozens of the farmers parked and abandoned their biggest tractors on the busy highway, creating an impenetrable roadblock.

I stood in the crowd of angry farmers taking notes and making pictures. When they realized I was a reporter covering their "strike," a couple of them puffed up and approached me with bad intentions. An impressively large deputy sheriff saw what was developing. He muscled through the throng of angry men and escorted me out of the mob.

Road graders from the state highway department attached chains to the parked tractors and dragged them off the highway. That road graders could actually tow those behemoths surprised me. With their brakes locked, the tractors didn't roll, they bounced along behind the graders.

Along Come the Kids

During our first year in Poplar Bluff, Sharon and I rented a comfortable two-bedroom apartment on the ground floor of a fourplex not far from our jobs downtown. Our daughter Katie was born on the anniversary of George Washington's birthday, February 22, 1975, while we lived in the apartment. She suffered from colic, which meant Sharon and I suffered, too. Katie wailed her lungs out for several hours every evening for a couple of months. Except for that, she was precious. After the colic, she was perfect.

(I painted my canoe olive drab during the time we lived in the apartment. I intended to use it to hunt ducks on nearby Lake Wappapello. Until I painted it, the canoe had faded from silver to tarnished-aluminum gray. Another one of the reporters at the DAR and I hauled the canoe to Lake Wappapello several times after work to fish. Sometimes we'd float through Poplar Bluff on Black River. I mention painting the canoe only because it has always been dull green to my children and grandchildren. It was silver when it dumped me into Locust Creek a few years earlier.)

A year or so after moving to Poplar Bluff, Sharon and I bought our first house, a square two-story that had been built early in the 20th century. A rickety garage leaned away from the alley out back. We spent much time and money updating the interior of the house, including installation of two wood-burning stoves, one downstairs and one up, and rebuilding the upstairs bathroom. You can blame me for the results.

Justin was born on Labor Day, September 4, 1978, after we moved into the house. (I witnessed and took pictures of the births of both of our children at Lucy Lee Hospital, where Sharon worked.) We had attended classes to prepare for the births, so I knew how to breath during delivery. Keeping busy with my camera distracted me from Sharon's ordeal. (Years later the hospital on the edge of downtown closed, and the Poplar Bluff Police Department moved into the building.) Justin didn't have colic. He had a crossed eye. He wore a patch over his other eye and a tiny pair of glasses. When he was nine months old, minor surgery corrected the crossed eye.

Unlike many women, Sharon loved being pregnant. It showed, too. She glowed.

During our years in Poplar Bluff, we spent many weekend days floating in canoes and inner tubes on the magnificent Current River. Nights we spent in a tent in campgrounds near Van Buren or Doniphan, two small river towns less than an hour's drive from Poplar Bluff.

After more than six years with the *Daily American Republic,* it became obvious that my newspaper career would not advance if I remained there. Sharon had left the hospital but had a solid nursing job with the Ozark Foothills Home Health Agency, but she also was ready for a change. Katie was now five years old, Justin almost two. We decided that if I could get a job that paid more than I was earning at the *DAR,* Sharon could take a break from work and be a full-time mom. She could not do that under our current circumstances. We needed two incomes.

By the time we left Poplar Bluff, I apparently had developed a bit of a southern Missouri accent. Every time I visited my sister Karin in Iowa, she started talking like Scarlett O'Hara from "Gone With the Wind."

CHAPTER 22

A MAJOR MISMATCH

I sent photos and resumes to newspapers around Missouri and Iowa and applied for positions advertised in *Editor & Publisher* magazine and *Publisher's Auxiliary.* The newspaper in Council Bluffs, Iowa, *The Daily Nonpareil,* needed a city editor. (Nonpareil means *without equal.* The printing industry used the word to describe a tiny type size.) Sharon and I drove to Council Bluffs for my interview with the newspaper's management. I accepted their offer. We moved in the summer of 1980 into an apartment a mile from downtown Council Bluffs, where the newspaper had its offices and production equipment.

So began the worst year-and-a-half of my working career. To begin with, *The Nonpareil* paid me a thousand dollars less than I had been told it would. As city editor, I was nothing more than a proofreader of the local news the staff produced. Those issues, plus oppressive surveillance and constant chipping from my bosses, soon convinced me to escape that situation as soon as possible.

The Nonpareil was owned by a chain of newspapers headquartered near Chicago that was notorious in the industry for its stinginess toward its employees and its products. I had left a small, family-owned daily newspaper that kept up with technology and equipment to join a newspaper that still used typewriters, gluepots and pencils to prepare copy for the typesetters.

At the *Daily American Republic,* we had used computers to write copy and set type for a couple of years before I left.

Paranoia Prevails

The Nonpareil had a handful of good young reporters to cover the region. Across the Missouri River, in Omaha, lurked the *World-Herald*, a newspaper of considerable size and prestige. It had one full-time reporter covering Council Bluffs. While I fully recognized it was incumbent upon *The Nonpareil* not to let *The World-Herald* beat it on any news from southwest Iowa, in particular Council Bluffs, the management's paranoia over this possibility cast a pall over our newsroom. Discussion at our daily news meetings routinely focused on what *The World-Herald* might report rather than on what we would be covering.

As city editor, I had zero input. I was in charge of page three of each day's edition. That's where local news went, regardless of its importance to our readers. Marching orders came from headquarters in Illinois. National and international news would dominate page one every day. Local news went on page three. That was the rule. How in the world, I thought, could suits in Chicago possibly know what was most important to readers of *The Nonpareil*? My instincts and experience as a university-trained and six-days-a-week reporter and fill-in editor counted for nothing.

I told Sharon I had to get out. She understood.

While we lived in Council Bluffs, my stepmom, LaVelle, still in Grinnell with Dad, died of pancreatic cancer in a Des Moines hospital.

I Lie to a Reporter

My military service led to an anecdote at *The Nonpareil*. The very unpopular Vietnam War remained fresh in people's minds. Protests against the war had erupted on college campuses and in cities all across the country. The military, and those who had served recently, more often got cursed than welcomed home.

We had a solid group of half a dozen writers in the newsroom. One of the reporters, a young woman, asked me about my military service. After I told her a little about what I had done in the Navy, she asked, "Are you ashamed?" All I could do was say "No" and turn back to work. The fact is that I was and still am ashamed of my part in the Vietnam War. Edges have worn off that shame, and I don't think about it much anymore, nor lose sleep like I sometimes did. It was a long time ago.

The source of my shame isn't so much that I opposed the war and served in spite of it, but that I took advantage of an opportunity. Although I missed Sharon deeply, I considered my Navy service an opportunity and an adventure. I saw places and did things that most people never will. As mentioned earlier, I knew serving would qualify me for the GI Bill, which would pay for my college education. I was a mercenary; I went to war for money. My service contributed to years of misery and suffering for people that I had no animosity toward. That legacy does not make me proud. It's why I seldom wear the "Vietnam Veteran" ball cap my brother the Marine gave me.

Time for Change, Again

My unbearable work situation in Council Bluffs convinced me that this might be the perfect time to pursue my dream of publishing my own newspaper. I discussed that idea with Sharon. She agreed that I should not stay in a job I hated. When I told the management at *The Nonpareil* that I would be leaving soon, they replied that my performance had been less than they expected, and it was probably best that I retreat to the countryside where my talents would fit better. They felt I had not been up to the big-boy newspaper scuffles of the city. My tongue had teeth marks for some time afterward, but I escaped that daily bush-league grind of frustration without biting it off.

Sharon, Katie, Justin, JoJo and me in front of the house we bought in Oregon, Missouri. A few months after this photo, I buried the puppy in the backyard after running over him in front of the house. Telling the kids broke my heart.

CHAPTER 23

RENOVATING A NEWSPAPER

efore notifying *The Nonpareil* that I was leaving, I had launched a search for a newspaper to buy in Missouri. During my days with the *Daily American Republic* in Poplar Bluff I had become acquainted with the Missouri Press Association. Now I sent a note to Doug Crews, editor of the Association, along with a brief classified advertisement to put in the Association's membership publications.

Not long after my "Newspaper Wanted" ad ran, a response arrived from the editor and publisher of a tiny newspaper. The *Oregon Times-Observer* served two little towns in Northwest Missouri. The weekly, tabloid-size paper actually resided in a trailer in Forest City, an even smaller town three miles west of Oregon. The owner said she put Oregon on the nameplate because Oregon was the seat of Holt County. She wanted the revenue from publishing county and city legal notices required by the state.

The forlorn little newspaper contained a few club and church items, feature stories about local history, and virtually no photographs or advertising. A shop a couple of hours away in Kansas produced and printed it. The publisher sent typewritten stories to the printer, who did the typesetting and layout. She mailed the *Times-Observer* in brown bags on which she had written the addresses of her readers. I learned later that she had inflated her number of subscribers by several hundred. Most of the people she mailed papers to never paid for it.

Our Paper's Lone Asset

The *Times-Observer* had one thing going for it – "legal" status. Missouri statute requires counties to publish probate notices, foreclosures, election notices and sample ballots in a "legal" newspaper. In order to be "legal," a newspaper has to have a Periodicals mailing permit from the Postal Service, an office in its place of business and a list of subscribers. A newspaper had to have been published for three years to qualify for a Periodicals mailing permit.

The *Times-Observer* had all that. Legal status meant it received a small but almost guaranteed monthly cash flow from the county. Even so, I called Robert Wilson, publisher of the weekly newspaper in Milan, Missouri. Wilson was a friend of the Stewart family, which several years before had moved from Brookfield to Milan.

"Should I buy the *Times-Observer*?" I asked him.

"No," he said without hesitation. He based his response on Oregon not having enough people or businesses to support even a tiny newspaper. Also, the farming industry of North Missouri, the backbone of the region's economy, had already begun to decline, a result primarily of the consolidation of small farms into big ones. Nearby I-29 made St. Joseph and Kansas City an easy drive for anyone itching to shop. Retailers in Holt County struggled mightily for a bit of the residents' spending.

With some down-payment help from Sharon's family and cashed in life insurance policies, we bought the newspaper anyway. Price, $12,000. We made quarterly payments for five years. Failure had never occurred to me. When we shared our plan, Mom asked me if Sharon knew what she was getting into. "No," I responded, "but she soon will." (Before Sharon and I approached her parents for a small loan, I had asked Mom if she could help. She said she didn't have any ready cash available. I don't think Bob ever knew that I had asked Mom for a loan before going to Sharon's family.)

Oregon, a community of nine hundred, didn't have a robust housing market. A local insurance agent who handled most of the local real estate deals showed Sharon and me the available stock – three houses. (The businessman became a steady advertiser in our newspaper.) We arranged a loan and moved into a small ranch-style house with an unfinished basement on an acre of yard on the southern edge of Oregon. (Several years after we left Oregon, fire destroyed the house.)

Half of the basement, after finishing, became the new office of the *Times-Observer*. Sharon and I quickly began making arrangements, as much as we could afford, to bring the newspaper into the 1980s. We called the publisher of *The Daily Forum* in Maryville, forty miles north of Oregon. His newspaper had a production shop and printing press. Sharon and I went up for a visit.

We had ordered a Compugraphic IV typesetting machine, a process camera to produce screened photo prints and other darkroom equipment, but it would not arrive for several weeks. The publisher of *The Daily Forum* didn't just agree to print the *Times-Observer* for an extremely reasonable price. He gave us a key to his building and said we were welcome to use the darkroom and typesetting machinery after his staff had gone home.

Commuting to Maryville

Several times a week for two months during the summer and early autumn of 1981, Sharon and I gathered news, photos and advertisements during the day and drove to Maryville to set type and lay out pages in the shop at *The Daily Forum*. Katie and Justin, then six and three, went along. They played until bedtime, then snuggled into sleeping bags on the floor of the *Forum* newsroom and went to sleep. This exhausting routine continued until the delivery of our typesetting machine and darkroom equipment. We continued to have our newspaper printed in Maryville for several years. I got out of bed early on Wednesday mornings, just a few hours after "putting the newspaper to bed," and drove to Maryville.

We did not have the equipment needed to process our pages into plates for the press. The backshop staff at *The Daily Forum* photographed the pages and burned the printing plates. It took only a few minutes for the press crew to print 1,500 copies of the *Times Observer*.

Sharon and I typed all of the news and feature stories, which we then retyped into the Comp IV to produce the columns of type. I also "set" the type and did the layout of virtually all of the advertising. We received very few "camera ready" ads. I also spent a couple of hours every Tuesday afternoon and evening processing photos. The film had to be developed, pictures printed and then reshot on the process camera to create the screened images needed for the page negatives that would be used to burn the press plates. Darkroom work took much longer than it should have because I reprinted photos repeatedly to get a print that would reproduce well and look decent in the newspaper. In addition to this extra time, a great deal of expensive photo paper ended up in the trash.

Gathering the News

While my frustration with the darkroom mounted, I could hear Sharon calling her list of elderly ladies from the Extension clubs, social organizations and church groups to get their "news." These reports often related who had opened the meeting with prayer and who had brought refreshments and what they were. We did our best from week-to-week to make these "community news" items read more like news stories than scrapbook entries. The meetings had little news value, but they did get local names into the *Times-Observer*.

Sharon fueled my frustration by chatting with each of these ladies about their aches and pains and their families' aches and pains until an anguished "aaaarrrrgggghhh" erupted from the darkroom. Sharon assumed

I was struggling with a particularly difficult photo and ignored me. She got to know many of the ladies well and developed neighborly relationships with most of them, many of whom she had never met in person.

"Community news" items don't get the play or the respect they once did in weekly newspapers. They should. They contain names of local people in items other than the police or court report. For years I carried in my wallet the clipping of a brief letter to the editor of a nearby weekly. A long-time reader, an elderly woman, wrote that she had sent in an item about her recent trip to visit relatives. The newspaper had not printed her "news." "Who do I blame for that?" she wanted to know.

Another publisher acquaintance often shared his favorite anecdote about community news. One of his "country correspondents," the people who gather and submit community columns, included something like this in her weekly report: "Mr. and Mrs. Charles Jones went to visit her sister, Mrs. Mable Smith, last Saturday afternoon. No one was home."

In a small community newspaper, names are the news.

Touring the County

My week started early Monday with a visit to the local school building, which housed kindergarten through twelfth grade. I stopped in the principal's office, chatted with the superintendent and then tried to corner a coach or two. After that I headed to Mound City, the largest town in Holt County, thirteen miles north of Oregon. Mound City, which was in the center of the county and logically should have been the county seat, had its own weekly newspaper, the *Mound City News*. The same family had published the newspaper for many years.

This is the Compugraphic IV machine we used to generate all of the type for the Times-Observer. Small newspapers around the country used machines like this for several decades, before computer "pagination" came along. As soon as we could afford it, we bought the word processor at left so we could type our stories and edit them before sending them to the Comp IV for printing of the type. The small machine that applied hot wax to the back of the type can be seen against the wall to the right. The wax held the type on the paste-up pages, but allowed strips of type to be moved if necessary.

The Mound City paper tolerated my incursion by ignoring me. I gathered news from the schools and city hall there and a bit of advertising. After gathering the Mound City news and ads I drove another six miles to the tiny community of Craig at the north end of Holt County. School and city officials there provided an occasional story, but the few businesses provided virtually no advertising to support my efforts. I drove to Falls City, Nebraska, and then down to Hiawatha, Kansas, once a month attempting to round up business. I abandoned those trips when it became apparent that they were wastes of precious time and gasoline.

Sporting events, both high school and junior high, and meetings of the school board, city council and county offices took time, as did weekly visits to many of the businesses in Oregon, Forest City and Mound City.

Occasionally through the years someone would come up to me at a ball game or a meeting and say, "You really get around. I see you everywhere."

The Weekly Routine

We dedicated Monday evening through late-night Tuesday to writing news, putting ads together and laying out the pages. A common edition of the *Times-Observer* had eight to twelve broadsheet pages. As our advertiser list grew, we more often had twelve pages. A photo feature page or a page with "signatures" guaranteed a twelve-pager.

"Sig pages" contained only the names of area businesses that wished everyone a Happy Valentine's Day, Blessed Easter or Bang-Up Fourth of July. We created sig pages to congratulate school teams on their winning seasons and to spotlight high school graduates every spring. We charged businesses only a few dollars to be listed on a sig page, so they were easy sells by phone. Many regulars agreed to let us put them on the pages without calling them. We published some thin journals, but almost every word and every photo in them originated in Holt County and related to it.

The forty-mile drive to Maryville on Wednesday morning sometimes followed only three or four hours of sleep. The final leg of the trip ran straight north on Highway 71. Once, after turning onto the highway, a drowsy thought occurred to me: "The road goes straight for several miles, so I can take a short nap." The edge of the highway jerked me back to reality. I shook myself awake, opened my window and turned up the radio.

When I got home from having the paper printed, Sharon and I sat at the dining room table and glued address labels on the upper corner of each paper. We bundled and sacked them according to postal routes. I then delivered bags of newspapers to the post offices in Oregon, Forest City, Mound City, Craig and Maitland. While making this run, I took papers to a number of grocery and convenience stores around the county. They sold papers for a quarter, of which they kept a dime. After we got our mailing list set up for the Forum's addressing machine, I could drop papers at the various post offices on the way back to Oregon. While I was delivering to the post offices, Sharon took papers to the two Oregon grocery stores for counter sales.

Katie and Justin helped put labels on the papers when they were home. Katie later started clipping ads for billing. About this time, she decided she wanted to go to college when the time came. She didn't know what she wanted to study, but she knew she didn't want to clip newspaper ads all her life.

Change of Direction

When *The Daily Forum* in Maryville got a new publisher, she raised substantially the cost of printing our paper. The higher rate probably would actually generate a profit for her. I called other newspapers in the region with press rooms. Through our membership in the Northwest Missouri Press Association, we had become acquainted with the publisher of the *Cameron Citizen Observer*. He gave us a price for printing that I'm sure profited him very little, if any. My Wednesday-morning trip changed from forty miles northeast to sixty southeast. The Cameron newspaper shop printed the *Times-Observer* the last two years of our time in Oregon.

A few years later, after Sharon and I had moved to Columbia, the Cameron publisher died young of colon cancer. A short time before his death, during a phone conversation with him from my office in Columbia, he admitted, "I ignored the warning signs."

In addition to the newspaper he published, the man left behind a young wife and several young children. Many Cameron citizens and newspaper people, Sharon and I among them, also mourned him.

Big News Nearby

Skidmore, Missouri, is a tiny village twenty-five miles north of Oregon. We moved to Oregon soon after the July 10, 1981, killing of Ken Rex McIlroy in Skidmore. For years McIlroy had terrorized the citizens of the town and the surrounding area. He died, as the book title says, *In Broad Daylight*, while sitting in his pickup truck on the main street of Skidmore. Someone fired a high-powered rifle bullet through the rear truck window into the back of McIlroy's head.

The award-winning book by Harry N. MacLean became a *New York Times* bestseller.

Just as area law enforcement couldn't bring McIlroy to heel, it couldn't find a witness to his killing. Although virtually everyone in the community knew who shot McIlroy, nobody would rat out the local hero. In addition to *In Broad Daylight*, a compelling read, the killing of Ken McIlroy led to countless newspaper articles, magazine features, other books and more than one film. It dominated conversation around Northwest Missouri for months.

Northwest Missouri Press Association

Sharon and I met many of the newspaper publishers in our region through membership in the Northwest Missouri Press Association, a regional affiliate of the Missouri Press Association. We saw many of them only once a year, at the association's annual January meeting in St. Joseph.

We all had the same love of newspapers and suffered the same problems that go along with small-town publishing: rising postal rates, finding competent help and scraping more advertising out of our perpetually shrinking rural markets. (The internet didn't exist yet, so that medium's assault on newspapers had not yet begun.)

The Northwest Missouri Press group soon jostled me onto its board of directors. My turn as president came in 1987. Later, when I went to work for the Missouri Press Association in Columbia, the newspaper people from Northwest Missouri remained close to our hearts. Through the years, Sharon and I caroused with them from time-to-time at press meetings, and I visited by telephone with them occasionally. It was always good to hear how they were doing.

At one of those Northwest Press meetings in St. Joseph, I heard a member of the *St. Louis Post-Dispatch*, a newspaper famous for its connection to the Pulitzer family, speak at a session. A member of the audience asked the speaker the correct pronunciation of the name. The speaker said he once overheard a member of the Pulitzer family answer that question: "It's like opening a door. You pull it sir."

Media people make me grimace when they mention the Pee-U-litzer Prize.

Cursed Typos

The last thing I wrote each week, often after midnight, was my weekly column, "Dear Mom." Exhaustion on top of my readiness for the week's production marathon to be over resulted in typos, especially in Dear Mom.

Our typesetting machine, the bulky blue and gray Compugraphic IV, displayed only one line of typed copy at a time. Misspelled words, grammatical errors and punctuation problems had to be recognized and corrected before you typed in the next line. Before we got an actual word processor that allowed editing of stories before sending them to the typesetting machine, I got good at composing stories on the Comp IV without previously pounding them out on the typewriter. Inevitably, when composing stories on the fly, one visible line at a time, errors slipped through the Comp IV.

Often, long after midnight on a Tuesday, when I was proofreading every story, cutline and ad in the paper, Sharon would hear "dang it!," or something like that, maybe a bit crustier. Another typo.

Lines of type with mistakes had to be reset, waxed, cut apart with an Xacto knife and stuck on top of the offending lines of type on the paste-up pages. Every page, with news, headlines and ads, had several different type fonts on it. Each font had its own film strip that fit into the Comp IV, so errors often required changing the font strip. All of that took more time, and this chore occurred just before putting the paper and Sharon and me to bed. We were tired and on edge. Sharon rocked. Every time she heard me curse during proofreading, she'd calmly respond, "just fix it."

Those mistakes would be corrected of course, without her input, but it made me proud to know that Sharon wanted the paper to be as clean as we could make it. Sharon doesn't have super powers, she is a super power. And very tolerant. But here's a tip: If you buy a weekly newspaper, keep your mouth shut while proofreading. You'll get to bed sooner.

Dog Food Dump

Holt County butted against the Missouri River five miles west of Oregon. Two miles west of Oregon, loess hills fell abruptly to the river bottom land. Forest City clung to the base of the hills. A massive concrete elevator, owned by Cargill at that time, rose up from the edge of Forest City. At harvest season grain trucks lined up away from the elevator, waiting a turn to dump their corn or soybeans.

When a harvest produced more grain than the adjacent railroad could haul away, a mountain of yellow grew beside the tracks on the elevator grounds. Holt County farmers, like others around the Midwest, grew soybeans, corn, a bit of wheat and alfalfa in the hilly countryside that covered two thirds of Holt County and the vast bottom land on the western third between the loess hills and the river.

Sometimes the river grew out of its banks and flooded the bottoms. I took Justin along on a trip to take pictures of a flood. On the way we came across a highway accident. A semitrailer hauling Alpo dog food had crashed off the Interstate 29 bridge over Highway 59 two miles north of Oregon. A road grader was pushing thousands of cans of dog food off the road. A news photo bonus!

I pulled over and got out my camera. As I stood beside the road, the grader ran over a can and shot Alpo all over my shoes and pant legs. Justin laughed as I wiped off what I could with weeds from the ditch.

We got back in the car and drove up to Mound City on the Interstate and then west past Bigelow toward the flooded bottom. Highway Patrol troopers manned a roadblock to keep people from driving into the floodwater. A couple of police dogs kept the troopers company. I got out to take some pictures and immediately attracted the attention of the dogs, who sniffed my shoes and pants with enthusiasm. Justin laughed again. I explained to the officers why their dogs were so interested in me. They laughed, too.

Several years later, after we had moved to Columbia, during another Holt County flood, a trooper and his dog lost their lives near that spot. Nobody saw what happened. Authorities concluded that the dog got into the water, and the trooper tried to save it.

A few miles south of the roadblock, the flood washed out a railroad trestle over a ditch south of Big Lake. That rail line carried several long coal trains every day – full cars heading south, empty cars north – through the Holt County river bottom and past the Forest City grain elevator. Power plants in the southeast region of the country depended on that coal from Wyoming. The day after the trestle washed out, the railroad shipped barges, cranes and other equipment up the rails to Big Lake. Coal trains soon resumed highballing past Forest City.

CHAPTER 24

NATIONAL TRAGEDIES

A s at other times, tragic events stamped themselves in my memory during our years in Oregon.

On July 17, 1981, two pedestrian skywalks collapsed and fell to the lobby floor of the Hyatt Regency Hotel in downtown Kansas City. One hundred fourteen people attending a popular afternoon tea dance died. *The Kansas City Star* received a Pulitzer Prize for its coverage of the tragedy.

On October 23, 1983, I had just pulled into the parking lot of a bank in Mound City on my regular ad run when I heard on the radio about a bombing in Beirut, Lebanon. American military personnel, mostly Marines, were there as peacekeepers during the Lebanese Civil War. The suicide attack on their barracks killed 241 of them.

On January 28, 1986, a volunteer crew of local handymen worked installing counters and plumbing in the new T.J. Hall Community Building across the street from the Courthouse in Oregon. I was driving there to make a photo for the paper. As I turned onto the downtown square, a radio announcer told me the space shuttle Challenger had exploded just after launch. All seven aboard, including school teacher Christa McAuliffe, perished.

Newspapers Matter

As much as anything, two brief anecdotes from our years in the hamlet of Oregon, Missouri, demonstrated to me that people appreciate their community newspapers.

On a Wednesday, about six in the morning, I was taking our newspaper pages to Maryville for printing. As I drove down Main Street in front of the courthouse, a local businessman-about-town stepped out of the telephone office and waved me down. He told me the huge concrete grain elevator at Forest City had split open and several people were buried in corn. I turned around, drove to the site, got a picture, gathered what information I could in a few minutes and headed to Maryville. The Maryville editor, whose crew labored busily on that day's edition, didn't leap on my offer, but I told him he could use the picture of the broken grain elevator if he would let me use his darkroom.

The photo in our paper bumped a page one picture of a woman with a quilt she had made. I don't know if *The Daily Forum* ran the picture. Nobody was killed at the grain elevator, but the story went on for several years as lawsuits progressed. The best memory about that incident, for me, was the local character stepping into the street to stop me as I headed out of town. I can still see him doing that.

Another time, the local International Harvester implement dealer promoted his pancake day in our newspaper. He bought a full-page ad inviting everyone in the county. A full-page ad made the week for the *Times-Observer*. The implement dealer ran a quarter-page ad every week, like many of our advertisers as much to support the newspaper as to sell their wares.

To my horror, I had left the date out of his pancake ad.

I immediately drove to grovel before the implement dealer. He scarcely looked up from his paperwork. He said simply: "A person who never makes a mistake isn't doing much."

His casual dismissal of this major error surprised me, but he realized something I didn't. His ad didn't need the date of his pancake day. Or a time. Or even a place. That full-page ad could have read simply "Free Pancakes!" As it happened, the line for pancakes slowed traffic on the highway. Word gets around in a small town.

People in rural communities where they know the people they read about, including themselves, appreciate *their* newspapers. They cuss the newspaper for many reasons, hollering the loudest when it doesn't arrive on time. One old saying about community newspapers goes like this: "People don't read the paper to get the news, they read it to see if the paper got it right."

CHAPTER 25

OPPORTUNITY KNOCKS

At the January 1989 annual meeting of the Northwest Missouri Press Association in St. Joseph, Doug Crews, the editor at the Missouri Press Association in Columbia, asked me if I would come to work for the association. Bill Bray, the executive director of the association at that time, was going to retire at the end of the year. Crews would succeed Mr. Bray, and if I accepted the offer, I would be the new editor.

After some discussion, Sharon and I agreed we couldn't turn our backs on the opportunity. For some time we had been working harder and harder on the *Times-Observer*, and revenue wasn't growing as fast as expenses. Sharon and I working together essentially earned only one modest income. Our children in a few years would be closing in on choosing post-high school paths, and we hoped that meant college.

Sharon had been away from nursing, a profession she loved and excelled at, for almost ten years. If we moved to Columbia, with its several hospitals, she would certainly land a good job. With her salary and what the Press Association offered me, we could manage college for the kids. I called Crews and told him I'd be honored to work for Missouri Press Association.

Fortunately for us, it didn't take long to sell the *Times-Observer*. A local woman and her son, who worked for the newspaper in Mound City but lived in Oregon and Forest City, found out we were trying to sell the paper. They bought it soon after we put it on the market. Unfortunately for Missouri

Press Association, it had another person on staff on June 19, several months sooner than expected.

At my desk in the Missouri Press Association building in downtown Columbia near the end of my twenty-five-year tenure there.

So began twenty-five years of serving Missouri newspaper people and working for the premiere newspaper association in the world. Missouri Press Association's building sits across the street in downtown Columbia from the first (and many claim the best) School of Journalism in the world, where I had struggled to earn my degree in 1974, fifteen years earlier. The privilege of working for Missouri Press Association and my experience as a daily newspaper reporter and small-town editor and publisher guided me through each day.

Boone Hospital Center, which is owned by the county, hired Sharon. After several years working patient care, Sharon moved into a nursing admin-istration position. She became the professional practice coordinator, working to ensure the hospital kept up with the cutting edge of patient care proce-dures. In the final years before she retired, Sharon helped coordinate Boone

Hospital's effort to earn its second and third Magnet status designation, the pinnacle of international recognition of nursing practice excellence.

Like telling me to "just fix it" at the *Times-Observer*, Sharon succeeded in helping to make her hospital among the best of the best.

CHAPTER 26

CIVIL WAR STREAK

ivil War reenacting captured my attention in the early 1990s after I read the book *Landscape Turned Red* by historian Stephen W. Sears. That fascinating, readable nonfiction book published in 1983 examined the battle called Antietam by the North and Sharpsburg by the South. Typically, the North named battles after nearby geographic landmarks; the South after nearby towns.

The September 17, 1862, battle at Antietam Creek near Sharpsburg, Maryland, was the bloodiest day in American history. Federal troops commanded by Gen. George McClellan repulsed an invasion of the north led by Gen. Robert E. Lee. By the end of that day, almost 23,000 men had been killed or wounded or were missing in the action at The Cornfield, Bloody Lane and Burnsides' Bridge.

Although President Abraham Lincoln castigated Gen. McClellan for failing to pursue the reeling Rebel army back across the Potomac River into Virginia, the tactical victory allowed the president to issue his Emancipation Proclamation when 1863 began. He had determined to free the slaves in the rebellious states, but he needed a military victory after so many unexpected, ruinous defeats in the first year-and-a-half of the war.

Fighting With the Fifth

I joined the Fifth Missouri Infantry – Confederate States of America, soon after reading the book about Antietam. Re-enactors in Central Missouri had organized the rebel unit; it was available, I joined. Having grown up in Iowa – a solidly Yankee state in the 1860s – joining a gray unit felt weird. But I had lived in Missouri – a solidly divided state in the 1800s – for many years. Back then, some Missourians owned slaves. A territory known as Little Dixie reached along the rivers of the eastern part of the state. This offered just the sort of curious situation that attracted me. I plunged in.

Like many other reenacting groups, the Fifth Missouri could "galvanize" and portray troops from the Union when necessary. Mock battles make a better show when the sides have nearly equal numbers. I participated in Missouri events at Boonville, Columbia, Fulton, Fayette, Carthage, Macon, Glasgow, Cape Girardeau, Athens and Washington. A few members of the Fifth, me in the bunch, marched in a governor's inauguration day parade on a frigid day in Jefferson City, and reburied the remains of Jesse James in Kearney, Missouri. I fired powder in fake battles in Kansas, Kentucky, Tennessee and Arkansas.

The Fifth Missouri Regiment participated in a reenactment in Glasgow, Missouri, during a brutally hot August. My wife, Sharon, and daughter, Katie, borrowed period gowns and attended a Civil War ball with me on the grounds of a mansion near our encampment. Earlier that day, a young reenactor and his girlfriend exchanged marriage vows in a ceremony among the tents.

In Gettysburg, Pennsylvania, a ghost awaited me at a special gathering.

All suited up and ready for battle during a cool-season reenactment. Being a rebel had never occurred to me before my interest in the Civil War blossomed. I would have preferred a Union unit. The Fifth Missouri was handy.

Hollywood Audition

At my first reenactment, at Butler, Missouri, the Fifth Missouri had a photograph made of the regiment. Our unit manager sent the picture to a production company lining up troops for a movie with the working title "Killer Angels." Movies with Civil War battle scenes rely on reenacting units to provide soldiers, troopers, canons, horses and all the appropriate gear. As a bonus for film-makers on budgets, reenactors provide their own housing, the tents they erect at their own exhibitions.

A few months later, the Fifth Missouri received word that the movie producers accepted its application to participate in the filming of "Killer Angels." Apparently, we looked authentic enough. Our ragged, baggy shirts obscured middle-aged bellies, some of them anyway, mine among them. None of us wore feathers in his hat.

Gettysburg Campaign

Reenacting friends and I crammed our gear into my Ford van (really, Ford Econoline) and headed east in the summer of 1991. We visited Antietam Battlefield Park on our way to Gettysburg for the filming. Many Civil War battle sites have been destroyed by development. The park at Antietam preserves the landscape as it was on the day of the 1862 carnage, from the Dunker Church to the Sunken Road to Burnside's Bridge.

To set the stage for our activities, you need to know something about what we were going to help to recreate. You'll meet the ghost soon.

Casualties in the slaughter at Gettysburg far exceeded those at Antietam, but the battle in south-central Pennsylvania raged over three days, July 1-3, 1863. Antietam's gore required one day. At Gettysburg, of the 95,000 Federal troops engaged, about 25,000 were killed, wounded or missing. The Rebel army of 75,000 suffered even worse losses, 28,000.

Fighting at Gettysburg, ten months after Antietam, ended General Lee's second and final invasion of the North. Historians refer to the battle at Gettysburg as the turning point of the Civil War, although the horror continued for nearly two more years. And Ulysses Grant's capture of Vicksburg, Mississippi, at the same time as the Gettysburg repulse, effectively sealed the deal for the Union. Confederates had suffered a crippling blow in the

North and lost control of the Mississippi River in the West. The cause of the South, whatever it claimed that to be, was lost.

The movie the Fifth Missouri was going to be in, titled "Gettysburg" when it opened in theaters across the country in 1993, is based on a historical novel written by Michael Shaara. Anyone with the slightest interest in American history would enjoy Shaara's gritty tale, *The Killer Angels*. The book won the Pulitzer Prize for fiction in 1975. Before arriving in Gettysburg, we thought the film would be titled "The Killer Angels." Producers changed the title to "Gettysburg," probably for marketing reasons.

Background Artists

In the movie, Martin Sheen portrays General Robert E. Lee, commander of the Rebel army. Jeff Bridges plays Joshua Chamberlain, one of the Union heroes at Little Round Top. Other stars in the film whose names you might recognize are Stephen Lang, who played General George Pickett, Tom Berenger and Sam Elliott. The producers didn't put my name on the posters or the marquees, but they did put it along with the names of every other reenactor in an attractive commemorative booklet about the filming of the movie. (Several people with the last name "Ford" participated and are listed in the column of names in the booklet. The name "Kevin Ford" appears under my name in the column. That was my younger brother's name. He wasn't there.)

We Fifth Missouri soldiers were "background artists," which means just what it says, people in the background. We are in the Pickett's Charge scene near the end of the movie. About 3,000 re-enactors were filmed advancing across land adjacent to the actual hallowed ground of the Gettysburg battlefield. The National Park Service refused permission to march on the ground that Pickett's Charge immortalized. During the real Pickett's Charge, on July 3, 1863, twelve thousand Confederate soldiers advanced through cannon fire across a mile of pasture to the gate of hell. Pickett's Charge petered out at the Bloody Angle. Except for minor skirmishing later that day, it ended three days of carnage.

The town of Gettysburg built an industry out of the history of the battle. That history includes President Abraham Lincoln's address delivered several months later during the dedication of the cemetery created for the Union dead.

During the July 1991 week we were in Gettysburg, I enjoyed watching the dynamics of filming more than the tedious marching forward, straggling back and marching forward again and again in the blistering heat. But the marching beat out the boring periods of idleness as cameras were repositioned to record different angles of the same scene.

In the real war, the Confederates prefaced Pickett's Charge with an hour-long barrage of fire from a hundred cannons. The film crew captured some of the thunderous, chest-thumping chaos of that scene with camera drones hovering in front of the canons as they spewed fire and smoke. Cool stuff.

An army of background artists awaits the beginning of filming of Pickett's Charge for the movie with the working title "Killer Angels." The movie is based on a novel by that name. It opened in theaters with the title "Gettysburg."

The Fifth Missouri is among the troops marching across the field and in the climactic battle scene at the Bloody Angle. If you know where and when to look you can spot my back, for about a second. Andy Warhol was wrong. Not everyone gets fifteen minutes of fame. I hung back from the chaos at the production company's makeshift Bloody Angle, determined to escape with my aged skull and bones intact. Other units of reenactors spent time in Gettysburg that summer for the filming of other battle scenes.

Tent City

Thousands of reenactors from all around the country pitched their tents in an orderly campsite a half mile from where the Pickett's Charge filming occurred. All of those tents, pitched side-by-side in ranks and rows, made an impressive site. A couple of dozen porta-potties in a row and thousand-gallon plastic tanks full of warm yellow Gator-Ade on flatbed trailers added anachronism – and an unappetizing juxtaposition – to the panorama. Southern Pennsylvania baked in the summer sun. Semi-trailers carried locker rooms where most of us showered at least once during the week.

Like every other reenactment I attended, idle chatter, jokes and lies filled the evenings around our campfires. As the nights grew longer, talk about the real battle of Gettysburg dominated the conversation. Ghost stories born during that three-day cataclysm got prominent play. Those anecdotes, some trifling, others hair-raising, fill books. They primed me for my spectral encounter.

CHAPTER 27

CRIME VICTIM

After a day of marching back and forth in the punishing heat, I craved a shower. Back in my tent, I stripped off my wool coat and pants, pulled on shorts, grabbed shower gear out of my campaign box and headed for the mobile locker room. After maneuvering through the coil of naked and near-naked bodies in the trailer, I stuffed my clothes and brogans (shoes) into one of the little lockers.

The shower perked me up, but I was sweating again before I got out of the steamy trailer wearing only shorts and sneakers. When I got back to my tent, I realized I had left my brogans in the locker. I hurried back to the shower trailer, hoping I had simply overlooked the shoes in my rush to escape the trailer. No such luck. My shoes were gone.

A foul mood descended upon me. "Why would a fellow reenactor steal another guy's shoes?" I had no evidence that my brogans had been stolen, but they were gone. We had a thief among us.

A more important thought then occurred: How was I going to participate in the filming without shoes? If the film crew didn't spot my sneakers and banish me from the set, the other guys in my outfit certainly would. Many soldiers marched and fought without shoes in the real war, but they were much younger than me and more dedicated to their mission. My tender, aged feet would object to marching unshod.

Spooked Into Action

I pouted late into the night, my irritation allowing little sleep. Reveille came well before sunup. Soldiers grumbled, crawled out of their tents, scratched, farted, formed into their units and marched the short distance to the breakfast tent. Not me. Still fuming and feeling sorry for myself, I curled up in the darkness and tried to go back to sleep. After breakfast the men marched out to the field where the make-up crew waited to smear greasepaint on hundreds of shiny faces.

Silence descended on the camp, deserted except for me with my bruised crime-victim psyche. Then, footsteps approached. Seconds later the sound stopped and a flap on the front of my tent flew open with a ripple of canvas. I looked up from my pallet, expecting to startle a thief, perhaps *the* thief.

Instead, I gazed upon a shape, entirely black, in what appeared to be a long overcoat and a flat wide-brimmed hat. The shape looked at me darkly, without eyes or any other facial features. I didn't move, just stared at the figure that appeared to be staring at me. The figure abruptly closed the tent flap and strode away.

I laid my head down, not understanding exactly what I had seen or how to respond. If it was indeed a thief, I determined to challenge him. I jumped up and dashed out of my tent into the weedy pathway that served as our street. Nobody was there.

I went back into the tent and laid down on my pallet, trying to figure out what had just happened. Perhaps influenced by the campfire ghost stories, I concluded that an Army officer from the past had come back to scrape up malingerers to throw into the coming battle. After seeing me, the officer grew disgusted, angrily tossed back the flap of my tent and stalked off, full of contempt for the cowardly slacker he had discovered.

I'm No Malingerer

Fantastic as it was, that conclusion shook me. Not only because I may have seen a ghost, but because I didn't want a military officer, even if he was a ghost, to think I was shirking my duty. It occurred to me that my childish pouting over stolen shoes somehow dishonored the thousands of men who had suffered on this field so many years ago. A pretentious thought perhaps, but it moved me. How could I let such an insignificant circumstance poison my spirit so much?

Sutlers' tents clustered nearby, providing the military mob with various gear, trinkets and provisions. At this hour, none were open. I went to the lounge tent. There a man sat alone eating breakfast off a plate in his lap and watching the news on a small television set.

"Do you know when the sutlers open," I asked.

"I'm one of 'em. What do you need?" the man asked.

"Do you have any brogans?"

He didn't have many, he said, but would be happy to check his stock for a pair that might fit. The shoes he found came a bit short in the toe but plenty wide. They would do.

"Will you take a credit card?"

"Sure!"

My budget for this expensive trip did not include eighty dollars for shoes, but without them my movie career would end before it began. I laced on the stiff brogans, gathered my gear, grabbed a cold biscuit from the chow tent and hustled out to where the film crew continued dabbing dirt on faces.

I'm still grateful to that specter for reminding me to keep troubles in perspective. Things don't always proceed smoothly or work out the way I want, but feeling sorry for myself just turns me into a sourpuss. Stuff happens. Get over it.

The movie company reimbursed background artists based on how far we had driven. Pay call ended the Fifth Missouri Regiment's participation at

Gettysburg. I got $56, cash. We broke camp and headed home. I declared to my traveling companions that I hoped the movie came out before I died.

After a couple of more years of reenacting, my enthusiasm waned. The hobby took too much time away from home, particularly on weekends, and way too much money. The Civil War had been fought largely by teen-agers, and it had been several decades since I was one of those.

Oklahoma Atrocity

Around the time I gave up reenacting, a young man parked a rental truck in front of the federal office building in Oklahoma City. When it exploded, the bomb inside the truck blew away the front of the building, killing 168 people, children among them.

An elegant monument erected on the site of the building reminds us of that vicious act of domestic terrorism that occurred on April 19, 1995. The federal government executed the bomber. One of his helpers remains in prison.

I think of that horrible act whenever I hear someone say we need to spend more millions protecting our country from foreigners. The Oklahoma City bomber was born and raised in the United States.

My Dad Dies

A rare lung disease (bronchiolitis obliterans organizing pneumonia – BOOP) struck my father early in 1998. He was admitted to University Hospital in Iowa City. He died there on January 30, age 84. Doctors had told those of his children who could gather, including me, that Dad had little chance to recover. I agreed with my siblings that the breathing tubes and machinery should be removed. My sister Candace spent many hours with Dad in his final days.

That spring, I joined my brothers Scott and Kevin for a round of golf at Oakland Acres, a few miles west of Grinnell. Dad played there several days a week after he retired, weather permitting. He'd go to the course early in the morning, fish in one of the ponds until his golf buddies showed up, then tee off with them. Dad's freezer always had crappie and catfish in it that he had caught at the golf course. He towed a shack to one of the ponds in winter and caught crappie through the ice. His shack sank in a nearby lake once. When the lake refroze, Dad raised the shack out of the water using car jacks. When he was 75, Dad shot his age on the golf course, a seldom-reached goal among amateurs. A few years before he died, Dad made a hole-in-one on the seventeenth hole, the only ace of his life.

During our round of golf, my brothers and I spread Dad's ashes between the seventeenth green and the nearby pond where he had spent many hours fishing. We tossed back shots of whiskey in Dad's memory, then advanced to the eighteenth tee.

CHAPTER 28

SITES OF THE SOUTHWEST

G iving in to whims that surface in daydreams can lead to grand adventures. Sharon and I experienced one of those in the year 2000.

Our children, Katie and Justin, had graduated from Hickman High School in Columbia and gone on to college. Sharon and I took advantage of our empty-nest status and took a road trip to the Southwest in the mid-90s. On that trip we visited the Grand Canyon, which planted in me a seed that sprouted into a life highlight.

We explored other sites in the magnificent Southwest during that trip. We've often stumbled upon spectacular pockets of natural beauty on our road trips just by looking at a map of the area we're passing through or by reading signs along the highway. Google helps, too. Sharon and I both love to explore the natural beauty of the countryside, most of which flies past quickly if we never leave the interstate.

Because it is only a couple of miles south of Interstate 40, Walnut Canyon just east of Flagstaff, Arizona, provided a convenient travel break. The short hike around the canyon's interior delighted us. A bit later we enjoyed the scenic drive from Flagstaff to Sedona. We hiked among the red hills around Sedona and explored other points of interest in the territory.

Then we visited the Grand Canyon, which isn't close to anywhere. The bleak landscape along the road north loses its attraction after a few minutes. I began to wonder if the canyon was going to be worth the drive.

There's a movie named *Grand Canyon*. I've seen it but don't remember much about it other than a dysfunctional family hits a wall. Each character thinks his or her life stinks. One of the parents decides everyone needs a time out. The one in charge says, "We're going to the Grand Canyon." Nobody wants to go, but they all want an escape, so they reluctantly climb into the family car.

The final scene shows the family arriving at the Grand Canyon, still scowling and carping at each other when they bother to engage at all. They walk as an agitated group to the rim of the canyon and look out over it. "Wow" hits them, deflating their complaints. Fade out, the end. That's my recollection of the film. It may not be accurate.

The Grand Canyon hit me like that. I didn't fade out, though. The view just planted the seed of a grand adventure.

Later, during a visit to Milan, Missouri, to see my mother and stepdad, I told Mother I hoped to hike down Grand Canyon someday. "You better do it before you get too old," she said. I took that casual advice to heart.

Making Plans

Early in 2000 I called the National Park Service reservation office to book a stay in Phantom Ranch at the bottom of the Grand Canyon. A nice woman who sounded young said 2000 was booked. It would be well into the next year before we could camp at Phantom Ranch.

"Name and address?" she asked.

"I live in Columbia, Missouri," I said.

"Columbia!" she exclaimed. "I know Columbia. I went to MU for a year. Loved it!" she said.

My call had injected interest into her day. She perked up and engaged. We chatted.

"Phantom Ranch reservations need to be made a year ahead," she said.

"Any cancellations?"

"I'll check," she said. "We do have a cancellation, but it's in July, the hottest time of year."

"We'll take it."

I did not want to wait a year. Heat we could deal with.

Sharon and I started training in March, sooner than necessary, but we didn't know that at the time, and I didn't want either of us to poop out half-way through this adventure. Sharon balked. After I emphasized to her what we had signed up for, a long downhill and then uphill hike in extreme heat, she got on board. We needed the exercise anyway.

Training For the Trek

Each morning, before sunrise and work, we walked a few blocks from our house to a street that descends steeply for a block, turns left and climbs steeply for a block. With four gallons of water in a backpack for weight, I walked in the street up and down those hills in the dark. Six times up and back. Every day. Sharon walked along on the sidewalk.

My Grand Canyon hiking research instructed me to make sure to train downhill as well as uphill. Repetitive downhill walking strains shins. Another tip: When hiking downhill, lace your shoes more tightly near the toes than at the top; on the hike up, lace your shoes more tightly on top. This technique helps prevent your toes or heels from grinding into your shoes on each step.

We paid too much for special shoes to make the hike; any solid walking shoes or quality sneakers would have done well. We wore our hiking shoes every day while training. The expensive shoes and thick socks served us well, though. Neither of us had any foot issues during training or the hike.

CHAPTER 29

OUR GRAND ADVENTURE

When the date of our trip arrived, around the Fourth of July holiday, Sharon and I flew to Las Vegas. Sweating, heat-weary tourists packed the sin city strip shoulder to shoulder, block after block. A clerk at our hotel explained. Las Vegas during summer usually is not crowded because of the heat, she said. On the July 4 holiday, however, Los Angelenos flee their city and mob Vegas.

"Los Angeles must be deserted," I said.

We climbed into our rental car and headed for the Grand Canyon. We drove over Hoover Dam to Williams, Arizona, then turned north for the hour's drive that seems like three through the desolate plains to Grand Canyon National Park. I had made a reservation for a room in the main lodge, a luxury we treated ourselves to, just because. We checked in and explored the South Rim area. Our hike into the canyon would start early the next day.

The day dawned as expected, clear with the promise of the usual July heat. Sharon and I rose early and slipped into our hiking clothes and our well-broken-in shoes. After a light breakfast we shouldered our backpacks and walked to the bus stop for the short ride to the head of the South Kaibab Trail. I was excited, borderline euphoric, with anticipation.

By the time the bus arrived several other people had gathered for the ride to the trailhead. The hike down on South Kaibab Trail would cover about eight miles. We would spend two nights at Phantom Ranch, then return to the South Rim via Bright Angel Trail, a hike of roughly nine miles. Many Grand Canyon hikers take this route, down South Kaibab and up Bright Angel, most of them descending and returning in the same day.

Sharon and I pose for a photo before beginning our descent of the South Kaibab Trail to the bottom of the Grand Canyon. With long sleeves and long pants, we looked different than the hikers in shorts and T-shirts. Our lightweight clothing kept us from baking in the sun.

Entering Wonderland

A modest crowd of hikers, including a group of Boy Scouts whose leader weighed too much for this hike even without the massive pack on his back, milled around checking gear before starting the descent. Sharon and I planned to take our time on the hike, stopping frequently for water and snacks. Nutrition breaks and my frequent stops to take pictures kept our pace slow.

The eight-mile descent to Phantom Ranch would take no more than six or seven hours. We had all day, and were determined to enjoy the breathtaking spectacle of the canyon. We soon found ourselves alone on the trail, behind the other hikers. The trail down among the red, orange, yellow, gray and pink rocks was unexpectedly smooth, from three to five feet wide, with occasional stone or log steps down steeper stretches.

South Kaibab Trail follows ridgetops for much of its length to the Colorado River, providing panoramic vistas of beauty, especially in the early-morning sunshine. For Sharon's sake, I had to maintain a measure of seriousness so she wouldn't think I was taking our challenge too lightly, but I felt like giggling. We had descended into wonderland.

About an hour into the hike we reached a plateau with a few scrub pines and convenient boulders for sitting. A couple of dozen hikers, including the Boy Scouts, gathered there to take in the scenery while getting a drink and a snack. We could see the trail ahead curving around a cliff and reappearing as a shrinking ribbon farther down the canyon. The valley home of Phantom Ranch showed narrow and green an impossible distance below.

Led by canyon wranglers, mule trains carrying material and people up the trail passed us as we picked our way down. At a spot a hundred feet above the river, an outcropping along the trail provided a shady spot to rest, although the temperature in the shade didn't fall much below one hundred. The rotund Boy Scout leader reclined in the shade, looking near death. He assured us he would be fine after resting, so we pressed on. By mid-afternoon we reached the footbridge across the rushing and rumbling Colorado River. A steady blast created by the clash of cold water and hot air blew dust off of us as we crossed to the bank on the north side.

Refreshing Mistake

Kaibab Creek, a shallow, narrow gravel-bottom run spilled into the river just beyond the pedestrian crossing. A hand-painted, weathered wooden sign beside a small pool in the creek encouraged us to "Cool Off, Wade In." We should have hesitated; alas, we did not.

Sharon needed to cool off, and she had no intention of hesitating. I on the other hand, flushed but fine, should have delayed at least long enough to remove the contents of my pockets – wallet, park papers, keys. All that stuff got cooled off along with me.

While refreshing us after our long hike, the frigid creek had a side-effect that we should have anticipated. Our calf muscles clenched up like fists. Deep massaging allowed us to march like a couple of kneeless robots the half mile to the office at Phantom Ranch. If the trail hadn't been level on this stretch, we would have had to await rescue.

Phantom Accommodations

Phantom Ranch has several tiny cabins for couples and families and two small bunkhouses for groups. Sharon and I had a cabin a few feet from Kaibab Creek, which cascades down the north wall of the canyon, through the flat of Phantom Ranch and into the Colorado River.

A long pipe of small diameter carries water from Kaibab Creek to the ranch for cooling buildings and irrigating the grounds. A smaller pipe connected our cabin to the main pipe. It delivered to the sink and the toilet, which occupied a small bumped-out addition on the side of the cabin. A hose dripped water in front of a fan in one of the cabin windows. That effectively cooled the interior of the cabin to a tolerable level. Two bunk beds, a small table and chair furnished our cabin.

While on the phone with the reservation person several months earlier, I had ordered the meals we would have at Phantom Ranch. Meals are served family style in a small dining area adjacent to the check-in office and the small souvenir and sundries area. We had two appealing-sounding choices for entrees, steak or beef stew. I ordered steak for one evening meal and beef stew for the other. Both meals raised our eyebrows. We had never had steak or beef stew that tasted like this. Peculiar. They were just food, that's all. We didn't request recipes.

The rules did include a happy surprise. It allowed the purchase of two beers per person per day. Being accompanied by a partner who doesn't drink more than a sip of beer held the promise of double delight for me. Our food reservation also included sack lunches for the hike up.

Exploring the Ranch

All material gets to Phantom Ranch by mule, all trash goes out that way. A helicopter landing space serves emergencies and special deliveries only. If you can't get yourself out of the canyon, you can pay $4,000 (the cost at that time) to have the helicopter fly you out. Even members of the ranch staff walk in and out. They hike down, work for several days and then hike out for time off. I asked one young woman how long it took her to walk out.

"I usually run," she said.

The day after we arrived at Phantom Ranch, we explored with sore calves the several acres of flat land around the Colorado River and Kaibab Creek. We hiked up the North Kaibab Trail until it began its steep ascent to the North Rim. Someone had waded to the far side of the creek and crafted a large salamander in the gravelly sand beside the stream.

We located the area across Kaibab Creek used for group camping. The Boy Scouts had spent the night there, but they already had packed out. A large clocklike thermometer hung on a post on the far side of the footbridge leading to the campground. Its hand pointed to 112.

Bright Angel

Our exploration of the ranch helped loosen our calf muscles, but they were still sore as we started the nine-mile hike up Bright Angel Trail after our second night in the cabin. The trail crossed the Colorado River, then followed it for a half mile before turning toward the escarpment and entering the cut of Bright Angel Creek. Unlike South Kaibab Trail, which tracks ridges for most of its length, Bright Angel Trail hides in the narrow, steep creek valley for several miles. This provides an altogether fresh perspective of the canyon's beauty.

Repeatedly during our frequent refreshment breaks, I wondered why people attacked a Grand Canyon hike as if it were a race, seeing how fast they could go down and back up. Perhaps they had hiked the canyon so often that the pure stunning beauty of it no longer moved them.

Sharon and I encountered few people on our hike into the canyon and even fewer on the way out. Most of those we did meet excused themselves and hurried past as if they were late for appointments. Our hike occurred before cell phones overwhelmed the world. I wonder if the Park Service now keeps records of how many people have been hurt from stumbling on canyon trails because they were texting. A selfie-stick could prove lethal to the unwary.

Disappointment

Near the beginning of the end of the hike out, almost to where a series of long switchbacks carries hikers up the steep cliff to the rim, a faint "chink, chink, chink" reached us from up ahead. We came upon a trail worker decked out in cowboy hat and boots, worn leather chaps, heavy leather gloves and a layer of dust. A horse and pack mule stood idly on the trail, looking for all the world like an 1849 gold miner's outfit.

The smallish person, a woman, early twenties-looking but sun-browned and rough, glanced at us briefly. She mumbled a return greeting. Using a pick she chipped flat chunks out of the surrounding rock to repair a section of the trail where mule trains stopped. The beasts must recognize their relief stations, because they use the same spots repeatedly. This creates shallow washouts in the trail that need to be repaired.

Sensing a not-hostile but certainly disdainful mood, we didn't linger watching the park employee work. This person displayed the same attitude we experienced on most of the canyon wranglers. They could do their jobs lots faster if all the citified tourists would stay out of their way. Maybe they're all doing community service. More probably they all embody the cowboy spirit and can't find a working ranch that pays as well as the federal government, and they resent it. Their universal surliness surprised me. Working even in that splendor gets boring, I suppose.

Another half mile up the trail, at a rest shelter, it struck me like a kick in the seat of my pants. I had neglected to make a picture of that totally authentic trail hand. Her attitude had put me off thinking about getting my camera out. I thought about hurrying back down the trail to ask if I could make a picture of her, but she likely had moved on. Missing that opportunity still rankles me, but I'm consoled by the thought that she probably would have told me to take a hike if I asked to take her picture.

At that rest area Sharon visited with a 90-year-old woman who said she had hiked in the canyon every year for many years.

Spectacular Sunset

The final push to the South Rim caused a problem for Sharon. All along the trail she had found hidden crannies or boulders to squat behind for relief. Nothing provided cover here. The trail winds back and forth on the face of the cliff in full view of all the hikers and all the tourists peering into the canyon from the rim. Compounding the problem, a sparse but steady parade of park visitors descends the trail for a short distance and then goes back up.

Sharon, abandoning our slow-pace strategy, beat me to the rim by several hundred yards. She used a restroom, then waited for me to surface. The final views of the canyon from the trail inspired me to stop for more pictures and video. I emerged reluctantly. Our hike in wonderland had ended.

We had a reservation in one of the modest dormitories near the canyon rim. After showering and resting for a bit in our room, we ate, then caught a crowded shuttle bus to Mather Point, billed as *the spot* to watch the sun set. A couple of hundred tourists gathered at Mather Point watching the sun disappear below the rim of the canyon. Behind them, the walls of the canyon burst into a palette with every brilliant color the bare earth has to offer. A spectacular finale for our Grand Canyon adventure.

Chapter 30

A Beautiful Day for Terror

Just as it did in New York City, September 11, 2001, dawned a beautiful late-summer Tuesday in Columbia, Missouri. I sat at my desk in my small office at Missouri Press Association responding to emails that had arrived overnight. The office manager poked her head through my door and asked if I'd heard what was going on in New York City.

"An airplane crashed into one of the towers of the World Trade Center," she said.

Missouri Press didn't have a cable television connection, but we did have a television set in the conference room that picked up a week signal from one of the local broadcast stations. I went to look. Most of the rest of that morning I could not take my eyes off the scene. It became obvious with the crash of the second jetliner into the towers, the crash into the Pentagon in Washington, D.C., and the airborne drama and tragedy of the fourth aircraft in Pennsylvania, that terrorists had struck a hard blow on America.

Watching the towers burn horrified me. Then the towers collapsed, engulfing several blocks of the southern tip of Manhattan in thick clouds of dust and debris. "Twenty thousand people work in those towers," I thought. "They all must be dead."

That possibility numbed me. Who hated America so much that they would kill themselves doing such a barbaric thing?

Ignorance Revealed

The attacks laid bare my naivete about the world, an innocent ignorance shared by most Americans and indeed by most people everywhere. I had considered myself moderately well informed about world affairs. Not so much now.

Terrorist attacks had happened regularly in various countries around the world, most often in the Middle East, but sometimes in Western, African or Asian countries. Genocide occurred, too, springing from cultural, religious or tribal hatred. Nothing approached the audacity of this strike, certainly nothing approaching it had occurred in the United States. Nothing I knew about the world explained what had happened.

Since then, reading books about the 9-11 disaster revealed to me that intelligence agencies in countries all around the world knew about terrorist groups and their potential for indiscriminate killing. Some of them knew they would strike the United States.

Those terrorists from Saudi Arabia and elsewhere in the Middle East had succeeded beyond their wildest imaginations. Not only did they destroy the Twin Towers, they made fear the prevailing emotion in American life and politics that continues to this day. That fear penetrated my psyche for a period. Americans were told repeatedly that we were on high alert and "if you see something, say something." We imagined terrorists lurking behind every tree. It reminded me of the fear of Communists during Joseph McCarthy's 1950s America.

Fear Denied

One day, soon after the September tragedy, I was walking to my pickup truck in the Missouri Press parking lot after work. An unfamiliar vehicle, another pickup truck, sat next to mine. I glanced into the bed of the pickup.

A dingy canvas backpack lurked in one corner near the tailgate. The thought struck me immediately that the rumpled pack could contain a bomb.

At that instant I realized the 9-11 attackers had scored a direct hit on me, 1,500 miles from Ground Zero. In the next moment I vowed to myself that those murdering zealots would have no influence over my life. They had opened my eyes to a sad, disturbing reality of today's world that must influence my perception of international relations, but they would not affect how I lived. The fear they desired to implant in America would not take root in me.

The United States and the world continue to deal with the aftermath of 9-11, with hundreds of thousands of people killed in wars in the Middle East and trillions of dollars poured into the pit labeled "national security." Politicians continue to wield those words like weapons when they want to whip up a crowd or buy a new war machine for the home of the brave.

CHAPTER 31

HONOR FLIGHT GUARDIAN

I n September 2010, it was my privilege to serve as a guardian for two World War II veterans on an Honor Flight to Washington, D.C. The two men had nothing in common, other than being Army vets. One lived in Ethel, a hamlet about eighty-five miles north of Columbia. He served in the South Pacific during the war, then worked as a self-employed handyman and ran a small business. My other veteran grew up in Columbia, Missouri, attended Harvard University, earned a Fulbright Fellowship and became a distinguished professor at the University of Missouri, where he taught for many years. He served in Europe, landing at Omaha Beach after it had been secured, and advancing on the left flank of the Army through France, the Battle of the Bulge and into Germany.

Those two men and I joined fifty-six other veterans and a crew of guardians on the Central Missouri Honor Flight. After a 2 a.m. buffet breakfast and briefing at a Columbia hotel, the group boarded two buses for the two-hour drive east on I-70 to the St. Louis airport. We flew to Baltimore. Two firetrucks pumped streams of water over the arriving plane to salute the veterans. Everywhere we went that day, groups of people welcomed the vets with cheers and ovations. Buses took us on a quick tour past the Capitol and the White House, then to stops at various military memorials in the area.

The Honor Flight program had started several years earlier because our country is quickly losing veterans of World War II. The program pays to fly vets to Washington so they can see the magnificent memorial to their service that was opened in 2004. Veterans of the Korean and Vietnam conflicts now are eligible to participate.

A wonderful reunion occurred for my veteran from Columbia. His granddaughter, who works in Washington, met him when he got off the bus at the World War II Memorial. She walked with him as he toured the memorial. Both wore wide smiles the entire time. The young woman, who expected to give birth to a son very soon, already had given the child her grandfather's name.

After witnessing a changing of the guard at the Tomb of the Unknown Soldier, our group returned to the Baltimore airport for the flight to St. Louis. During the flight, the veterans enjoyed a mail call. Honor Flight organizers had encouraged friends and family of the veterans, and other citizens, to write letters to the veterans. As our two buses drove past Kingdom City on the way to Columbia, more than fifty motorcyclists sped down the I-70 on ramp, roared past our buses and escorted the veterans back to Columbia. The Highway Patrol had blocked all traffic on I-70 and every entrance ramp between Kingdom City and Columbia. A cheering mob at the hotel welcomed the heroes home.

Almost four years later, my Columbia vet's obituary appeared in a local newspaper. He was 93. My vet from Ethel, I don't know about.

To Appease My Wife

Sharon insisted that I include other activities I've been involved with through the years.

"This is a memoir, not an autobiography," I say. "You can put that stuff in my obituary."

She scowls. I relent. So, to make her happy ...

In Oregon, Missouri, I led my son's Cub Scout den for a couple of years. Nobody else had time. We went camping a couple of times, made boot jacks and sawhorses, played games in the yard and went sledding when it snowed.

A couple of guys from Maryville came to Oregon one day and cajoled me into becoming the first president of a new chapter of the Jaycees. The motley crew we assembled managed to gather enough funds and enthusiasm to build an outfield fence on the ballfield at Forest City. My stint as president of the Northwest Missouri Press Association got mentioned earlier. When we left Oregon and moved to Columbia, I was in line to become president of the local chapter of Ducks Unlimited.

In Columbia, I've been president of the Optimist Club I've been a member of since 1989, president of Columbia Toastmasters, and a member of the board of the Tiger Quarterback Club. I've participated in several Clean-Up Columbia drives, Aquatic Restoration Plantings and invasive species removal efforts. For six years I've mounted a personal assault on the bush honeysuckle that chokes the woods in the city park behind our house. Every eight weeks, I donate blood to the Red Cross.

These and other small things are the least I can do for the community where I live. So many give so much; so many more give nothing, not even time.

Chapter 32

Newspaper Challenges Mount

Newspapers, especially those in larger cities, have struggled in the past twenty years with declining revenue and readership because of the internet, which blasted the methods of delivering advertising and news into countless digital fragments. Many other industries have felt the disruption of the internet, which has changed great segments of our lives.

Here's another issue that has hurt newspapers, but has implications far beyond them. More and more people read not much of anything. Mark Twain said something like this: "Those who don't read have no advantage over those who can't." Too many people read nothing. A vast number of those people who read nothing vote. Chilling to think about. Columnist and social critic H.L. Menken's comment went like this: "Half of Americans don't read a newspaper. Half of Americans don't vote. Let's hope it's the same half."

How to address the problem of aliteracy is anyone's guess. Newspapers have control of their products, and they can strive to make every issue so informative and entertaining that people will feel compelled to read them. Unfortunately, that costs money, more money than most newspapers can draw from their readers and advertisers.

Unless someone finds a way to get more Americans to read, the country faces a bleak future.

The Missouri Press Association headquarters in downtown Columbia, Missouri. In the right background are Jesse Hall, the administration building of the University of Missouri-Columbia, and the iconic "columns." The University's Academic Hall burned in 1892. The six columns in Francis Quadrangle were spared demolition after the fire and have become an iconic symbol of Mizzou.

Proud of the Privilege

I am proud to have worked in the only industry that the U.S. Constitution protects from the government. After the preamble, the word "press" is the twenty-sixth word of the Constitution: "Congress shall make no law respecting the establishment of religion, or prohibiting the free exercise thereof, or abridging the freedom of speech, or of the press ..." Speech and press are mentioned in the First Amendment because without them, all of our other freedoms would be gone in a flash.

It was an adventure to be a newspaper person, and it was a privilege to serve Missouri's newspaper people for twenty-five years. The Press Association honored me beyond my capacity to respond by inducting me into its Newspaper Hall of Fame in 2018. The ceremony was held in St.

Louis during the association's annual convention. Several members of my family, Sharon, our daughter and son and my mother-in-law, brothers Scott and Kevin and their wives, and sister Candace and her husband, honored me with their presence, as did John Stanard, my boss at the *Daily American Republic* in Poplar Bluff, and his wife, Vida. The presence of those family and friends made the occasion extra special.

30

Epilogue

Since my retirement from Missouri Press Association in 2014 and Sharon's from Boone Hospital Center a year later, we've traveled some in the United States and to several countries over the oceans. We both enjoy going, and we plan to continue doing that for several more years. We have no plans to leave Columbia. We like it here.

Katie, her husband Greg and their children, Nate, Aleah and Karsen, live in O'Fallon, Missouri, a western suburb of St. Louis. Justin, his wife Tami and their children, Olivia, Isaac and Elias, live in Maryville, Tennessee, several miles south of Knoxville. Sharon and I visit them occasionally through the year, and they often join us in summer and for holidays.

As I wrote in the prologue, my reason for writing this was to record for my family some of the interesting adventures and mundane details of my life. If others found this account entertaining, that's a bonus. I wish I had a volume like this about members of the Ford and Stewart families. Some of those people were characters to the core. Their stories that haven't already been lost will fade away with the passing years. That's unfortunate for them and for us.

Perhaps this memoir will encourage others to record some of their experiences for their families, for those who might be curious and for those of us who just like stories. Big picture historians miss so much. Each of us has a little history.